DEMEN EXPOSED

A Journal Of A Demon Deliverance Minister

By Rayford L. Johnson

Copyright © 2016 By ThugExposed.Org

Author's Note: The word "satan" is placed in lowercase throughout this book, for symbolic purposes out of respect to the Holy names of the true and living God, which are God the Father (Yahweh= God in Hebrew), Jesus (Yeshua= Jesus in Hebrew) and Holy Spirit (Ruach HaKodesh= Holy Spirit in Hebrew) which are in uppercase throughout this book.

Copyright Disclaimer: Under Section 107 of the Copyright Act 1976, allowance is made for "fair use" for purposes such as criticism, comment, news reporting, teaching, scholarship, and research. Fair use is a use permitted by copyright statute that might otherwise be infringing. Non-profit, educational or personal use tips the balance in favor of fair use.

ACKNOWLEDGEMENTS

I want to thank my Pastor and good friend Fernando Perez, for being lead by the Holy Spirit in taking the time years ago, to pray a deliverance and generational curse breaking prayer over me, and for teaching and training me in the healing and deliverance ministry.

I want to also thank my good friend Victor Torres for supporting ThugExposed.Org Ministries financially, prayerfully and with wise counsel. God has truly used Victor to keep our outreach ministry afloat and to expand, when at times it often appeared the ministry was financially on its last leg. I thank God for you Brother. I ask those who will read this book, to please support Victor's ministry at www.armed4battle.com. He is a very humble and anointed Christian author, speaker and 26-time World Arm Wrestling Champion.

I want to be sure to thank my weekly prayer partners Chaplain Bill Tamm and Derrick Stephens for their friendship, ministry support and accountability. Also Jail Chaplains Terry Toliver and Gary Cox and Juvenile Hall Chaplain Dan Thompson, for their support, training, prayer and encouragement. Also I want to say thank my long-time co-worker in journalism and friend Genoa Barrow, who edited and laid out this book and edited the *Thug Mentality Exposed* book.

There are just too many people, family and ministries that God has used to help inspire and to educate me to write this book. If you are reading this book and you are one of those people or ministries, thank you and may God bless you.

Most importantly I want to thank God for His mercy, grace and compassion for saving and delivering me from the grip of satan many years ago through His Son Yeshua Hamashia (Jesus Christ in Hebrew) so I could have eternal life and the awesome privilege to joyfully serve Him here on Earth.

God Bless,
Brotha Ray

TABLE OF CONTENTS

INTRODUCTION.. PAGE 1

CHAPTER 1- HISTORY OF SPIRITUAL WARFARE........ PAGE 8

CHAPTER 2- CASTING OUT DEMONS & BREAKING CURSES.... PAGE 13

CHAPTER 3- WHY DELIVERANCE IS NEEDED........... PAGE 15

CHAPTER 4- HOW DEMONS COME IN.................... PAGE 16

CHAPTER 5- SPIRITUAL LEGALITIES EXPLAINED..... PAGE 18

CHAPTER 6- HOW CAN SO MANY DEMONS FIT INSIDE THE HUMAN BODY? .... PAGE 23

CHAPTER 7- HINDRANCES OF DELIVERANCE.......... PAGE 27

CHAPTER 8- NO SURRENDER, NO DELIVERANCE.... PAGE 30

CHAPTER 9- BASIC PRAYER OF SALVATION & DELIVERANCE.. PAGE 33

CHAPTER 10- RECEIVING THE HOLY SPIRIT........... PAGE 38

CHAPTER 11- HOW TO START YOUR DAY IN THE LORD (Learning How To Hear From God): *Includes The Testimonial, "My Personal Encounter with the Demon of Sasha Fierce."* .... PAGE 44

CHAPTER 12- HOW TO MEDITATE ON GOD'S WORD...PAGE 90

CHAPTER 13- HOW TO SPIRITUALLY FIGHT................PAGE 97

CHAPTER 14- ANTICHRIST-NEW WORLD ORDER WEAPONRY... .... PAGE 108

CHAPTER 15- SIGIL MAGICK: THE DEMONIC POWER BEHIND SYMBOLS... PAGE 116

CHAPTER 16- UNDERSTANDING & SAFEGUARDING YOUR SOUL FROM THE NEW WORLD ORDER- OPENING HELL'S ABYSS- DEMONIC TECHNOLOGY & MIND-CONTROL: *Includes The Testimonial, "Demonic Origin of Playing Cards... Can They Cause Curses?"* .... PAGE 121

CHAPTER 17- OUR MIND WORKS LIKE A RADIO............... PAGE 133

CHAPTER 18- ANGELS ON ASSIGNMENT- GOD'S DIVINE PROTECTION........ .... PAGE 152

CHAPTER 19- PREPARING FOR THE HEALING & DELIVERANCE MINISTRY..... .... PAGE 168

DEMON MENTALITY EXPOSED

A Journal Of A Demon Deliverance Minister

INTRODUCTION

This book is only for those who are willing to commit to pick up their cross and follow Christ.

And he said to them all, if any man will come after me, let him deny himself, and take up his cross daily, and follow me.
— Luke 9:23

The Holy Spirit compelled me to write this book for the purpose of educating people on the inner workings of the demonic kingdom. It explains how demons are able to attack and disable Christians from their destiny in Christ and how current technology is already virtually wiring and programming humanity to accept the Mark of the Beast (666) and the antichrist's New World Order kingdom. This book will arm the Believer with information to safeguard themselves from the enemy's advance technological weaponry.

My people perish for a lack of knowledge.

Hosea 4:6

It will teach Believers how to maintain their deliverance and healing, by helping them understand the position and power that they have through Yeshua Hamashia (Jesus Christ in Hebrew).

Wisdom is the principal thing; therefore get wisdom: and with all thy

DEMON MENTALITY EXPOSED

A Journal Of A Demon Deliverance Minister

getting get understanding.

Proverbs 4:7

This book will also give the Believer the tools to win souls for the Kingdom of God, break curses and cast out demons.

I would like to thank my Pastor Fernando Perez of Fernando Perez Ministries, a true man of God, for mentoring and training me throughout the years on the area of healing and deliverance. I'm eternally grateful to God for his humbleness, support and willingness to help me establish my ministry in healing and deliverance.

DEMON MENTALITY EXPOSED

A Journal Of A Demon Deliverance Minister

History of Spiritual Warfare

Since that epic event, when satan known as Lucifer, a cherub angel at the time and his 1/3 of following angels were violently cast down to Earth from Heaven for their rebellion against God, satan and his minions have declared war on all of humanity.

And the great dragon was cast out, that old serpent, called the devil, and satan, which deceiveth the whole world: he was cast out into the earth, and his angels were cast out with him.

Revelation 12:9

Be sober, be vigilant; because your adversary the devil, as a roaring lion, walketh about, seeking whom he may devour:

1 Peter 5:8

Why? Because humanity is made in God's image, so when satan and his army looks at us, they see the image of their judge, who has already set judgement on him and his followers to be thrown into the Lake of Fire forever and ever.

So God created man in his own image, in the image of God he created him; male and female He created them.

Genesis 1:27

Therefore rejoice, ye heavens, and ye that dwell in them. Woe to the

DEMON MENTALITY EXPOSED

A Journal Of A Demon Deliverance Minister

inhabiters of the earth and of the sea! For the devil is come down unto you, having great wrath, because he knoweth that he hath but a short time.

Revelation 12:12

And the devil that deceived them was cast into the lake of fire and brimstone, where the beast and the false prophet are, and shall be tormented day and night for ever and ever.

Revelation 20:10

Jesus tells us that the Kingdom of Satan's mission is to: steal, kill and to destroy.

The thief cometh not, but for to steal, and to kill, and to destroy: I have come that they might have life, and that they might have it more abundantly.

John 10:10

The United States military is divided into various divisions and troops at various ranks. The Kingdom of Darkness operates within the same format, however, with more soldiers, experience, technology and with supernatural powers.

The good news is that God the Father out of his great love for us, sent His Son Jesus (Yeshua) to destroy the powers of Satan and his army.

DEMON MENTALITY EXPOSED

A Journal Of A Demon Deliverance Minister

He that committeth sin is of the devil; for the devil sinneth from the beginning. For this purpose the Son of God was manifested, that he might destroy the works of the devil.

1 John 3:8

Satan has created countless legions. A legion according to dictionary.com is: A division of the Roman army, usually comprising 3,000 to 6,000 soldiers.) Each legion has been assigned to create and inflict sickness, disease, murder, rape, depression, car accidents, divorce, gangs, substance abuse, drunkenness, child molestation, anger, lying, pride, adultery, false religions, music (secular), witchcraft, new age, rebellion, sexual perversion, greed, fornication, guilt, suicide, government, product creation (clothing, video games, TV shows, etc.), secret societies, doubt, confusion, insomnia, panic attacks, fear, scandals, pharmaceutical addiction, mind control, and the list goes on.

In order to be successful on their mission, they have to operate within God's spiritual law. Meaning they must operate in accordance to a human's freewill. This is why God warns us in His Holy Bible to not give place to the devil (Ephesians 4:27). Because practicing sin can open portals within a human soul and body, for demons to enter in. Like well-trained lawyers, satan and his demons are well versed in God's laws. They understand that His law says:

For the wages of sin is death; but the gift of God is eternal life through Jesus Christ our Lord.

Romans 6:23

DEMON MENTALITY EXPOSED

A Journal Of A Demon Deliverance Minister

Therefore satan and his demons know, that if they can tempt humanity to sin, then they can bring curses in a person's life legally, which will eventually lead to death.

This is why the Kingdom of Darkness is constantly tempting and influencing humanity to give place to sin. Because, it not only gives demons a legal right to operate in that individual's life, but even down their family bloodline, which is known as generational curses. Once one demon obtains entrance into a person's soul (soul = mind, emotions and will), they can open the door for their comrades to come in.

The term "gateway drug," is often associated with marijuana. The theory being that using marijuana over a period of time can eventually lead to a desire for stronger and more harmful drugs. Let me give you a spiritual interpretation... A demon obtains entrance into a person's soul through smoking marijuana, that demon that gained entrance into the body and soul, can later open the gate to allow other demons— such as depression, cocaine, laziness, etc.— to enter and curse the individual's soul.

The good news is that God did not leave His Believers helpless. Out of His love for us, He has given those who will to Believe, the Holy Spirit and spiritual armor to defeat the works of Satan and his demons.

But ye shall receive power, after that the Holy Ghost is come upon you: and ye shall be witnesses unto me both in Jerusalem, and in all Judaea, and in Samaria, and unto the uttermost part of the earth.

Acts 1:8

DEMON MENTALITY EXPOSED

A Journal Of A Demon Deliverance Minister

For the weapons of our warfare are not carnal, but mighty through God to the pulling down of strongholds;

2 Corinthians 10:4

Finally, my brethren, be strong in the Lord, and in the power of his might. Put on the whole armour of God, that ye may be able to stand against the wiles of the devil.

For we wrestle not against flesh and blood, but against principalities, against powers, against the rulers of the darkness of this world, against spiritual wickedness in high places. Wherefore take unto you the whole armour of God, that ye may be able to withstand in the evil day, and having done all, to stand.

Stand therefore, having your loins girt about with truth, and having on the breastplate of righteousness;

And your feet shod with the preparation of the gospel of peace;

Above all, taking the shield of faith, wherewith ye shall be able to quench all the fiery darts of the wicked.

And take the helmet of salvation, and the sword of the Spirit, which is the word of God:

Praying always with all prayer and supplication in the Spirit, and

DEMON MENTALITY EXPOSED

A Journal Of A Demon Deliverance Minister

watching thereunto with all perseverance and supplication for all saints;

Ephesians 6:10-18

This book is written as a spiritual warfare manual, to guide the Believer in creating a strategy through the Word of God, to put satan and his demons under their feet.

DEMON MENTALITY EXPOSED

A Journal Of A Demon Deliverance Minister

TESTIMONIAL

Sexual Soul-Ties

I remember getting a call from a friend of mine, asking me to go visit his cousin, Joe, who was in the hospital after overdosing on heroin upon being released from jail that week.

When I arrived at the hospital room, a pleasant, clean cut young woman greets me, she tells me that she is the girlfriend of the same man that had overdosed. I introduced myself as Evangelist Rayford Johnson and she informs me that she is a Christian and that she has been trying to get Joe to go on the right path. I look over and I see Joe laid out, but alert. Joe is tatted head to toe, with street and gang related tattoos. I introduce myself to Joe and begin to explain to them how drug addiction works from the spiritual side, and how it gives demons legalities to enter into a person.

I also explained other ways an individual can open up demonic portals for demons to come in, such as; tattoos, ungodly music and fornication. I then proceeded to boldly ask them if they had engaged in fornication, at which time, the young lady bashful nodded her head yes, as I could tell she was embarrassed. My intention was not to embarrass or condemn them, but to have them break all the spiritual legalities so they could be set free.

"The truth will make you free."

John 8:32

DEMON MENTALITY EXPOSED

A Journal Of A Demon Deliverance Minister

We then held hands all together with Joe laying in the bed. I begin to pray assuming Joe would manifest demons fairly quickly, however that did not happen. When I called out the spirit of fornication and the chief demon behind the sexual soul tie. The young woman started growling in a deep monstrous voice as she was looking down at the bed. As I continued to pray, her manifestation began to escalate and she is growling to the point where it could be heard in the hallway. Joe, at this time, is looking at me like, 'what did you do to my girlfriend?'

Her neck begins to pulsate violently as if there was something trapped inside, trying to get out. Her breathing begins to intensify and I feel compelled to grab the vomit container on Joe's bedside table and place it beneath the young woman. A few seconds after I did so, she collapses on the bed and vomits out a white, milky substance. She then begins to cry loudly stating, "what was that, that wasn't me, what was that?" Her crying then swiftly turned to joy. She knew Yeshua had set her free.

As far as Joe, I don't believe at that time he was fully ready to surrender to the Lord. Unfortunately, he was released from the hospital and headed back to the streets. I still continue to pray for him.

Notes:

DEMON MENTALITY EXPOSED

A Journal Of A Demon Deliverance Minister

—— PERSONAL DELIVERANCE TESTIMONIES ——

Inmate-Deliverance (County Jail)
(Back and Stomach Illness Healed in Jesus' Name)

It's me Ramiro —– inmate #———–I just wanted to write you and thank you for coming to see me last week. Well, let me say I was feeling sick for a few days and the day you came as well. It was crazy because when I walked in the room you were waiting for me, I even felt more sick. I was feeling really sweaty and was seeing stars like my head was spinning around.

Then you started praying for the demonic spirits to leave my body, I begin to feel chills all over my body. I even got really sad and began to cry. It was really what was happening, I couldn't control it. That made me believe in God even more. When you were done, I felt like I could run and jump or do whatever a 27-year-old man should be doing. (Before) I had felt like an old man, I couldn't get out of bed or nothing, I was giving up on hope.

So, if there are people out there that don't believe in you, I do brother! I was like that at one time, but I know what you do is true. I read my Holy Bible and share the word with those that want to hear it. I was an active Norteno (gang member) but I dropped out because I got moved on for a bad call, because these dudes were from Sac and I was from ————— , and I think back, 'what did I get from it besides going to jail or losing love ones and my family?'

Now I'm going to prison and I have not one of my so-called homeboys

DEMON MENTALITY EXPOSED

A Journal Of A Demon Deliverance Minister

send me a letter or pick up my calls. The only person that's here is my wife and family and God!!! He is for real and I will keep Him by my side for life. So, by that being said, I thank you for what you've done for me and taking the time to come see me.

Your Brother, Ramiro

DEMON MENTALITY EXPOSED

A Journal Of A Demon Deliverance Minister

Casting Out Demons & Breaking Curses

Mark 16:17-18

17 And these signs will accompany those who believe: in my name they will cast out demons; they will speak in new tongues; 18 they will pick up serpents with their hands; and if they drink any deadly poison, it will not hurt them; they will lay their hands on the sick, and they will recover."

In my teenage and early adult church years, I observed demons manifesting in people such as shaking, yelling, getting violent, and even laughing hysterically. At very rare times I have even seen preachers lay hands on the demon possessed and cast out the demons in Jesus' name.

I grew up hearing Bible stories of Jesus and his disciples casting out demons, however it was usually not presented as something applicable to life today. Yet, it was never explained to me why, it was just something most pastors and ministers did not want to talk about as a vital ministry for today. I have had pastors honestly admit to me that the demon deliverance ministry scares them. They conveyed that they feared the demons would jump out of the demon possessed individual and on to them.

I have been a licensed minister since 2005, yet did not enter into the ministry of healing and deliverance until 2007, which consisted mainly of reading a prayer over individuals. There was some effective results however, my intense training in deliverance did not start until 2013, when my pastor Evangelist Fernando Perez began train-

DEMON MENTALITY EXPOSED

A Journal Of A Demon Deliverance Minister

ing me in the ministry of deliverance. After a year of training, I was anointed with oil and commissioned in the ministry of healing and deliverance in Yeshua's name. Since that time I have been ministering healing and deliverance on a weekly basis and seeing God's miraculous power move in Yeshua's name.

When we look at Jesus and His disciples and the first church in Acts, we see deliverance ministry was a very vital ministry for the Kingdom of God. The first ministry assignment Yeshua gave to His disciples was to cast out demons.

One must understand that Salvation is when one is redeemed from satan's camp. However many are rescued from the enemy's camp, yet they are still in restraints and the shackles of sinful addictions, mental torment, sickness, generational curses etc..

Deliverance is the power God has given believers in Christ to break us free from the enemies shackles, in order for us to accomplish God's perfect will for our lives. Expecting a believer who has not been fully delivered to accomplish God's perfect will for their life, is like expecting a construction worker to perform his assigned task blindfolded with handcuffs and leg shackles on. Most of his time will be spent in frustration, stumbling all over the worksite, possibly injuring himself or even killing himself, it would be a miracle for him to complete the most simplistic task. This is how it is with many Christians after they receive Salvation, up and down in their Christian walk, frustrated about not knowing what God's will is for their life. Why? Because their soul was redeemed from the devil's camp, however the enemy's shackles were never fully removed. The objective of deliverance ministry is to break these spiritual shackles off.

DEMON MENTALITY EXPOSED

A Journal Of A Demon Deliverance Minister

The following training, is a guide for those who believe they have been called into the deliverance ministry:

Luke 9:1-6

9 Then he called his twelve disciples together, and gave them power and authority over all devils, and to cure diseases.

2 And he sent them to preach the kingdom of God, and to heal the sick.

3 And he said unto them, Take nothing for your journey, neither staves,nor scrip, neither bread, neither money; neither have two coats apiece.

4 And whatsoever house ye enter into, there abide, and thence depart.

5 And whosoever will not receive you, when ye go out of that city, shake off the very dust from your feet for a testimony against them.

6 And they departed, and went through the towns, preaching the gospel, and healing every where.

Why Deliverance Is Needed:

Sin is a spiritual fruit (Galatians 5:19), evil spirits/demons bring the seeds of the sinful fruit. Once the seed of sin is planted, more demons come to nurture that seed through temptations, opportunities, negative peers, music, false doctrine, etc., to bring that sinful fruit to fruition. You have to get the root of the fruit.

A demon once given a spiritual legality to enter into a person, cre-

DEMON MENTALITY EXPOSED

A Journal Of A Demon Deliverance Minister

ates a stronghold within. It's a lot easier for the demon to manipulate the soul (mind, emotions, will) from the inside, rather than the outside. The human body becomes an open residence for the demon and the demon's peers, which again can be in the thousands.

Demons are like computer hackers, they hack the mind and body to program sinful viruses and sicknesses into the mind and body. These viruses are tormenting and sinful thoughts and curses, some of which have come through the womb and bloodline through spiritual legalities for generations.

How Demons Come In:

Demons can only enter mankind through spiritual legalities. Those legalities come through sin and generational curses. Their mission is to get into the soul, in order to gain influence and access to the soul's three components, which are the mind, emotions and will. If they can influence the mind, then they can stir the emotions to guide the will to do satan's bidding. Satan's goal is to hijack the body, do missions with it and then crash and destroy it.

However he needs keys to steal the vehicle. These spiritual keys are the legalities. Some individuals, including Christians, just leave their soul doors open, with the key in the ignition. The majority of the Church has not been educated on satan and his demonic techniques to hijacking earthly souls and bodies. Satan influences mankind to create these keys which opens the doors to the soul. These keys are not recognizable to the average Christian.

DEMON MENTALITY EXPOSED

A Journal Of A Demon Deliverance Minister

Can A Christian Be Possessed By A Demon?

Note: Demons cannot possess the Christian's spirit, because the Holy Spirit dwells there. However if the Christian opens their soul's door through sin, ignorance or generational curses, demons can enter into the soul, which also gives access to the body.

Satanic Keys to the Soul: substance abuse (drugs & alcohol), sexual perversion, tattoos, New Age practices, generational curses, gangs, secret societies, astrology, yoga, martial arts, witchcraft, depression, traumatic experiences, unforgiveness, etc.

——— DELIVERANCE STORY ———

Demon Deliverance of a Teenage Homosexual

I was assisting at a healing and deliverance conference with my friend and one of my mentors Pastor Ron Barnes in Sacramento, California, when a 19 year-old, tall African-American kid comes in front of me for prayer, wearing a black T-shirt with a large image of Marilyn Monroe, an iconic female sex symbol from the 1950s.

I ask him, "How can I pray for you?" and he leans his head towards me and whispers, "I want to be delivered from homosexuality." I then place my right hand onto his tall Afro-hairstyle and began to pray, being led by the Holy Spirit. I begin to break generational curses, sexual soul-ties, calling out the spirits of rejection, neglect, abandonment, abuse, etc.. His body begins to sway back and forth and his knees begin to buckle a little. I then proceed to bind the strong man (chief demon) of homosexuality, LGBT, sexual perversion, and pornography and commanded them to manifest and be bound and go into the pit of hell.

DEMON MENTALITY EXPOSED

A Journal Of A Demon Deliverance Minister

At this point his large frame buckles over, yet he is still standing and then begins to cough violently, which is common when demons are being expelled out of a person. His knees then buckle more and he goes to floor still coughing and now groaning. He conveys to me that he feels heat and things moving through his stomach and chest area. As I continue to call down the fire of the Holy Spirit, he finally goes down from his knees to his back, like a prize fighter who got K.O.'d.

After about five minutes I help the young man up and he tells me he felt things lift out of him, including the spirits moving in his stomach and chest area. He conveyed to me as he was smiling in a joyful tone, that he felt really good and much lighter. We both began to thank Yeshua for his deliverance.

Spiritual Legalities Explained

Satan and his demons are legalists. The Word of God tells us that satan is accusing us day and night in the courts of Heaven.

And I heard a loud voice saying in heaven, Now is come salvation, and strength, and the kingdom of our God, and the power of his Christ: for the accuser of our brethren is cast down, which accused them before our God day and night.

Revelation 12:10

Then he showed me Joshua the high priest standing before the angel of the LORD, and Satan standing at his right hand to accuse him. The LORD said to Satan, "The LORD rebuke you, Satan! Indeed, the LORD who has chosen Jerusalem rebuke you! Is this not a brand plucked from the fire?"

Zechariah 3:1-2

DEMON MENTALITY EXPOSED

A Journal Of A Demon Deliverance Minister

Ephesians 4:27 tells us not to give place to the devil. In other words we have to give satan place. Let me give an analogy: Even the Chief of Police cannot just enter anyone's house and perform a search and arrest someone. There are laws and policies in place, even for law enforcement to abide by.

A citizen must do something or there must be a credible witness against the citizen, bringing assumption that they have broken or are breaking the law. That is the only way the police can obtain a search or arrest warrant. Without one, the police are breaking the law, and they will be held accountable.

The spiritual legal system works in a similar way. When we break God's law by sinning, it can give satan and his demons a legal right to bring curses, sickness and even death on an individual, even a Believer.

The wages of sin is death.

Romans 6:23

Afterward Jesus findeth him in the temple, and said unto him, Behold, thou art made whole: sin no more, lest a worse thing come unto thee.

John 5:14

"My people perish for a lack of knowledge."

Hosea 4:6

DEMON MENTALITY EXPOSED

A Journal Of A Demon Deliverance Minister

Many legalities of curses, diseases and premature death come into individuals through generational curses. Their ancestors were involved in pagan secret societies, witchcraft covenants or gangs, which paid to receive the earthly benefits from the demonic world through performing rituals such as worship to the Kingdom of Darkness, which includes oaths, ritual dances, incense burning, astrology and even animal and human sacrifices to these false deities.

Performing these types of abominable acts is a form of currency exchange between the individual and the Kingdom of Darkness, that places the person and their blood-line in a contract with the Kingdom of Darkness. In these rituals, often a son or grandchild is offered up to the deities in exchange for worldly riches, high positions or fame. Only the blood of Yeshua can pay and remove the individual from these contracts, which bring curses, sicknesses and premature death.

To break these demonic contracts, which are the legalities from the demonic contracts they had entered in or their ancestors had entered in, they must repent and renounce for the sins they have done and what their ancestors have done. Again satan and his demons are legalists, the proper spiritual legal motions must be implemented before the curses are broken. God honors his legal system and process with both parties, because He is a God of justice and integrity.

On the other hand, our God who is sovereign King over all the universes. His Holy court is the court of courts and He is the king of kings. His Word and law is final, it must be honored by all in this uni-

DEMON MENTALITY EXPOSED

A Journal Of A Demon Deliverance Minister

verse and in every other universe. When a Believer speaks His Word from the spirit-man which he birthed in every Believer which has received His Son Yeshua Hamashia as Savior and Lord, all creatures, demons, fallen angels and even satan himself must honor and obey it.

However we must speak His word legally, not illegally. Remember, there is a real court system in the spirit realm. This means if someone is asking God to meet a financial need in their life, and they use His legal word to petition Him by reciting Philippians 4:19 which states: "But my God shall supply all your need according to his riches in glory by Christ Jesus." Yet if they have unforgiveness in their heart against a brother, they have decreed an illegal petition to God.

And when ye stand praying, forgive, if ye have ought against any: that your Father also which is in heaven may forgive you your trespasses.

Mark 11:25

Satan and his demons will argue that they have the legal right to attack this Believer's finances, based on the Believer being in sin, which gives legal right for the Kingdom of Darkness to bring forth curses, due to the Believer operating as a citizen of the Kingdom of Darkness, which is under the law of sin, meaning they are subject to the same consequences, being under that kingdom.

An individual can be a citizen of the United States, however if they get caught with drugs in Singapore, they must face the same punishment as any other citizen in Singapore, even if they are a citizen of the U.S.

DEMON MENTALITY EXPOSED

A Journal Of A Demon Deliverance Minister

When an individual operates under the "law of sin," it can give legal right for satan and his demons to bring forth curses and eventually death. Again, in the Holy law book, which is the Holy Bible, it's stated:

For the wages of sin is death; but the gift of God is eternal life through Jesus Christ our Lord.

Romans 6:23

It's stated in God's Word in Revelation 12:10 that satan is our accuser, who accuses us day and night as a court prosecutor before the Holy court of God, looking for a legal right to attack a Believer. This is why Ephesians 4:27 tells us not to give place to the devil.

Going back to the Believer petitioning God's throne, they must first forgive and repent before their petition can become legal. Once it is legalized, they can now enter into the full rights of a citizen of the Kingdom of God.

Notes:

DEMON MENTALITY EXPOSED

A Journal Of A Demon Deliverance Minister

How Can So Many Demons Fit Inside The Human Body?

In Latin, spirit means breath. These spirits come in like breaths of air. Ephesians 2:2, states that:

2 Wherein in time past ye walked according to the course of this world, according to the prince of the power of the air, the spirit that now worketh in the children of disobedience:.

Almost everyone I have ministered deliverance to has reported after the prayer, that they feel lighter. You might ask, why is that? I read a study about research a university conducted on dying patients. During this study they placed hospice patients on a bed scale. When the patients would die, the scale would lift five-ounces, which is about the weight of a humming bird.

So the speculated conclusion was, the soul weighs approximately five-ounces. A demon is an evil soul, which seeks a human body to get rest in and to accomplish satan's will. So a soul is a measure of air. Air can move freely, expand, shrink and move through physical boundaries. Air can be compacted into small compartments. Souls, which are units of air, can be compressed in multiples within the human body. The Bible tells a story of a man with legions of demons within him. A legion according to dictionary.com is:

A division of the Roman army, usually comprising 3,000 to 6,000 soldiers.

So this clearly shows that 3-6 thousand demons have the ability to compress themselves into the human body. Remember, a soul has three components, which are the mind, emotion and will. Individuals have enough challenges managing just their own soul. Can you

DEMON MENTALITY EXPOSED

A Journal Of A Demon Deliverance Minister

imagine the oppression of the voices, thoughts, emotions and willful drive of thousands of these evil spirits? This is often the root cause of many cases of mental illness, unemployment, lack of education, anger issues, bipolar disorder, depression, suicide, etc..

Notes:

DEMON MENTALITY EXPOSED

A Journal Of A Demon Deliverance Minister

DELIVERANCE STORIES

Deliverance Of A Sorority Sister

A professional, college graduate, African-American woman in her mid 20s approaches me at a healing and deliverance conference, which my pastor, Fernando Perez was hosting, requesting prayer for depression, anxiety and some marital issues. Her husband stood right behind her. I felt lead by the Holy Spirit to ask her if she was in a sorority, she said "yes."

I know from my studying of Greek letter organizations and other secret societies, that they pay homage to false pagan gods through rituals, oaths, dancing, etc.. This gives demons a legality to enter into the individual and create curses down their family's blood line.

As I begin to pray, this professional woman's body begins to convulse, she begins to hiss like a snake with her tongue going in and out, eyelids fluttering, screaming periodically. Then all of a sudden she begins to laugh in a sinister tone almost uncontrollably. I know it's a spirit laughing through her. As I continue to pray for the Holy Spirit fire to burn these demons out of their hiding place and be cast out to the pit of hell, she begins shaking wildly and walking sporadically in circles.

When I had called out the demons behind her sorority, one specifically, Minerva, this woman faints to the floor. I was able to catch her and lay her down easy. After about a few seconds on the floor, she rolls over on her belly and begins to slither around like a snake, hissing with her tongue, with her back postured up, resembling a cobra in striking position. As I continue to order the spirits out in Yeshua's name, she then rolls

DEMON MENTALITY EXPOSED

A Journal Of A Demon Deliverance Minister

on her back and begins animating Egyptian tutting with her arms, still hissing like a snake.

(Note: Greek letter organizations derived out of the Egyptian and Babylonian culture, so this spirit's roots were being exposed as it was in full manifestation.)

At this point the Holy Spirit through word of knowledge is having me call out other spirits and to break various curses in her blood line on her mother and father's side, such as child molestation, freemasonry, sexual soul-ties, witchcraft, marine spirits, spiritual husband, etc..

After about five minutes of binding and ordering these spirits to the pit of hell in Yeshua's name, she begins to cough violently and then vomits up a milky white substance (which is common in demon deliverances).

She then stretches out and goes immediately into a deep sleep and I put a long towel over her to cover her up. After about 15 minutes, she rises her upper body off the floor looking around and her husband helps her up.

When I ask her about her experience, she has no recollection of how she was manifesting. She conveyed to me that she felt good, much lighter and happy, and that her mind felt clear. We all gave Yeshua, our Lord and Savior, all the glory for this amazing deliverance he did on this young woman.

DEMON MENTALITY EXPOSED

A Journal Of A Demon Deliverance Minister

Hindrances Of Deliverance

I want to present to you five things that will stop an individual's deliverance, which are:

1. Refusing to Forgive

And when ye stand praying, forgive, if ye have ought against any: that your Father also which is in heaven may forgive you your trespasses.

Mark 11:25

2. Refusing to Repent & Renounce

But your iniquities have separated between you and your God, and your sins have hid his face from you, that he will not hear.

Isaiah 59:2

What does it mean to truly repent and renounce? My fellow deliverance minister, Ron Barnes explains it the best way I have heard it, in his seminar training manual titled: *Warrior's Training:*

Repent: A change of heart (how you feel), mind (how you think) and direction (how you act); to be restored to your former high position in God.

Renounce: To take back a right or privilege previously given through an act, a vow or an open door; to change allegiances or allances; to reject an agreement.

DEMON MENTALITY EXPOSED

A Journal Of A Demon Deliverance Minister

3. **Pride**

Pride goes before destruction, and a haughty spirit before a fall.

Proverbs 16:8

4. **Jealously**

But if you have bitter jealousy and selfish ambition in your hearts, do not boast and be false to the truth. This is not the wisdom that comes down from above, but is earthly, unspiritual, demonic.

James 3:14-15

5. *Unbelief*

But let him ask in faith, with no doubting, for the one who doubts is like a wave of the sea that is driven and tossed by the wind. 7 For that person must not suppose that he will receive anything from the Lord;

James 1:6-7

Notes:

DEMON MENTALITY EXPOSED

A Journal Of A Demon Deliverance Minister

DELIVERANCE STORY

DELIVERANCE OF A GANGSTA RAP CEO COUNTY JAIL

I struck up a conversation at the County Jail with the CEO of a Bay Area record label. He told me he had just received 14 years for racketeering, but was grateful that God had mercy on him. He stated to me that he wanted to go into ministry. I asked if I could pray for him. He told me it was a coincidence, because he just told an inmate, "I need Rayford to pray for me to get some of these demons out of me." He stated he wasn't usually out of his cell at this time, but something told him to come out.

I obtained permission from the deputies on the unit, to go into a classroom to pray for him. He stated he had been tormented by a demon which causes him not to move while in bed and torments him in his sleep.

As I came against the demons of pharmakia, marijuana and the demon behind the Thizz music, among others, he said he felt something crawl up his spine and come out. As we went through the other areas casting demons out and breaking curses, he felt his feet getting really hot along with his his head.

At one point he felt something moving on his shoulders and in his chest. I asked the angels to remove it with their swords which they did. When I broke the spirit of cancer, he felt a knot form in his stomach, then a release. He began to get misty eyed, stating he felt good and so much lighter. I then imparted by the direction of the Lord, the same anointing that is in me, into him in Yeshua's name.

DEMON MENTALITY EXPOSED

A Journal Of A Demon Deliverance Minister

No Surrender, No Deliverance

There is a false doctrine of counterfeit grace, which is being preached to the world. This doctrine makes an individual believe that as long as they say a short Prayer of Salvation, they will receive fire insurance from the flames of Hell and can go on living in sin with no real obligation to truly repent and change, thanks to God's grace and mercy.

I often encounter in the field of ministry the self-proclaimed Christian gang member. Active gang members believing they are secure in God's Salvation, they base this on a short prayer of Salvation they once said. Their belief system tells them that they can maintain Salvation through ritual prayers, Bible studies and prayer services, etc.. Some have the belief they can even be divinely protected in their gang banging activities.

Ye cannot drink the cup of the Lord, and the cup of devils: ye cannot be partakers of the Lord's table, and of the table of devils.

1 Corinthians 10:20

The same applies for those involved in secret societies, Greek letter organizations and other pagan cultic groups.

Let me break this down as simply as I can:

The Prayer of Salvation, is the surrendering of one's self to the Lord Yeshua Hamashia (Jesus Christ in Hebrew) making Him Lord over every area of our life. If we continue in our sin, with no repentance, we have not made Him truly Lord over our life. Therefore there is no salvation.

DEMON MENTALITY EXPOSED

A Journal Of A Demon Deliverance Minister

If a gang member has not renounced his or her gang after confessing the Salvation Prayer, they have disqualified themselves from the gift of salvation. The two major requirements are--we must repent for our sins and forgive others, as God has forgiven us. Let me explain:

    A. A gang member who chooses to stay in their gang, can't repent, because being a gang member requires living in sin. To repent, means to turn from one's sin.

    B. A gang member can't truly forgive, because a gang member is fueled emotionally by having hatred and animosity towards his or her gang rivals. God says in His Word, he can't forgive those, who are not willing to forgive others. Therefore the gang member remains unforgiven, dying in their sins.

A gang is a demonic cult, invented by satan. When one joins a gang, they literally make a demonic soul covenant with satan. I pray for gang members who are tormented by evil spirits throughout the week. I have had evil spirits which have refused to come out. Not because the power in Yeshua's name was ineffective, but because that demon or demons had a legal right to be inside the individual, because the individual refused to renounce and leave their gang. Gang members have literally told me that they can hear the demon spirits tell them they aren't going anywhere as I pray for them. Every time, it's because the gang member refuses to renounce and leave their gang or forgive someone.

I had a gang member who was in this same situation, the next week he made a sincere decision to repent and renounce his gang, at which time I was able to cast the evil spirits out in the name of Yeshua Hamashia. Without those demonic voices and other manifestations, he finally had peace through the power of Christ.

DEMON MENTALITY EXPOSED

A Journal Of A Demon Deliverance Minister

Bottom line, demons of rage, murder, theft, sexual deviancy, addictions, witchcraft, generational curses, sickness, mental illness, etc. have a legal right in a gang member, up until the gang member or cult member renounces their ties and repents for their sins.

Matthew 12:43-45

43 When the unclean spirit is gone out of a man, he walketh through dry places, seeking rest, and findeth none.

44 Then he saith, I will return into my house from whence I came out; and when he is come, he findeth it empty, swept, and garnished.

45 Then goeth he, and taketh with himself seven other spirits more wicked than himself, and they enter in and dwell there: and the last state of that man is worse than the first. Even so shall it be also unto this wicked generation.

Notes:

DEMON MENTALITY EXPOSED

A Journal Of A Demon Deliverance Minister

Basic Prayer of Salvation & Deliverance

For God so loved the world, that he gave his only begotten Son, that whosoever believeth in him should not perish, but have everlasting life.

John 3:16

God is a loving and forgiving God who delights in His creation. In His Word He says, *"For I know the thoughts that I think toward you, saith the Lord, thoughts of peace, and not of evil, to give you an expected end."*

Jeremiah 29:11

Now think of the goodness of Yeshua... and repeat this prayer out loud...

Father, I decree your son Yeshua Hamashia as Lord and Savior over every area of my life. I believe Father, that your son Yeshua Hamashia was placed on the cross for my sins and the world's sins, and that He was buried and raised by You on the Third Day.

I repent for all my sins (name them) and for my ancestors' sins on my mother and father's side, known and unknown. I ask your forgiveness for all my sins and I forgive all those who have offended me and sinned against me. I forgive myself.

I renounce all demonic activity that I have participated in my past and my present, I renounce, reject and repent this day for all:

DEMON MENTALITY EXPOSED

A Journal Of A Demon Deliverance Minister

• Witchcraft, Sorcery, Black Magic, White Magic, Divination

• Pharmakia (Witchcraft through Drugs)

• Horoscope, new age, yoga, psychic readings, etc.

• Tarot cards & palm readings, and all cultic practices which pay homage to pagan eastern religions.

• Ouija Boards

• Worldly music & entertainment which pays respect and glamorizes evil lifestyles.

• Prayers to false gods and spirit guides.

• Membership in secret societies, Greek letter organizations, Freemasons, etc.. all organizations that give honor to false gods.

• Gang ties (name your gang)

• Soul ties-current and past, and all demonic unions created through fornication and occult sex magic & perversions.

• I renounce all demonic covenants, soul ties and portals to the soul, created through drugs, alcohol, strange tattooing and strange piercings.

By the power of the blood of Yeshua, I break off every curse, hex, spell, soul tie, curse words people have spoken, generational curses of disease, sickness, premature death, depression, addictions,

DEMON MENTALITY EXPOSED

A Journal Of A Demon Deliverance Minister

mental illness, anger, murder, divorce, gangs, violence, poverty, sexual perversion, witchcraft, abuse, abandonment, idolatry, jealousy, unforgiveness, pride, social life problems, _____,_____ in every area of my life. I call now the fire of the Holy Spirit (Hebrews 10:29) to burn and torment every demonic spirit hiding within my conscious and subconscious mind, emotions, body, tattoos, symbols, home, etc.. I command the Holy Ghost fire in Yeshua's name to burn them out of their hiding places now!!!

Angels of the Lord bind the demonic king and queen ruling over any area of my life and put a fiery chain around the neck of the head demon or principality who received the assignment from satan to afflict, torment, oppress, and possess me, and a chain of fire around every evil spirit under the authority of the principality.

Break their demonic crowns off their heads, along with all their jewelry, amulets, and any devices and weapons they came with on their assignment.

I command these spirits to pack their belongings right now and prepare to leave my body and soul. My soul, being, my emotions, will, and conscious and subconscious mind. Leave my home and family in Yeshua Hamashia's name... Now!!!. I say out!!! in the name of Yeshua!!!

Angel of the Lord, drag these spirits and every spirit under their authority into the outer darkness into the Abyss. Evil spirits, I command you never to return again. Yeshua, I ask you now to close every portal of my soul, that has been open to the demonic world through the sorcery I've done through drugs, alcohol, sexual promiscuity, worship of demons and false gods, generational curses, occult

DEMON MENTALITY EXPOSED

A Journal Of A Demon Deliverance Minister

magic, gangs, pagan secret societies, witchcraft, etc., and the spirits which have haunted my mind with tormenting thoughts, voices, hallucinations, nightmares, demonic paranormal experiences, sickness and disease, etc..

I thank you for the blood of your son Yeshua, I decree right now that it protects and covers me from the enemy. I thank you Yeshua for the stripes that you allowed to be torn violently in your back, for Your Word states in 1 Peter 2:24, "By His stripes we are healed." So I decree that by Yeshua's stripes, I'm healed, from the top of my head to the soles of my feet.

Father, Your Word says in Romans 10:13, "Whosoever that call on the name of the Lord, shall be Saved." and John 8:36 states, "Who the Son has set free, is free indeed." So I call on you, Yeshua Hamashia as my Lord and Savior, and I decree by Your Word that I'm set free indeed!!!

Father, I ask that you fill me now with your Holy Spirit. Acts 1:8 states that I will receive power when I receive the Holy Spirit and that He will lead me into all Truth according to John 16:3. I receive this Holy impartation by faith and the gifts that accompanies it, such as the gift of speaking in new tongues, among others which is referenced in scripture according to 1 Corinthians Chapter 12. Lord, I ask you to give me the discernment of every skill-set, talent and spiritual gifts you have placed within me, so I can utilize them to win souls and bring you glory. I decree by faith that your Holy Spirit is leading me now towards Your perfect will, plan and purpose for my divine destiny in Christ's Kingdom.

I decree that I have the mind of Christ according to 1 Corinthians

DEMON MENTALITY EXPOSED

A Journal Of A Demon Deliverance Minister

2:16 and the divine armor of God according to Ephesians 6, which is the helmet of salvation, breastplate of righteousness, belt of truth, sword of the spirit (which is the Word of God), and that my feet are prepared with the Gospel of Christ. I decree that I and my family are blessed in Yeshua Hamashia's name.

So Be it!!!!

Praise God!!!

DELIVERANCE STORY

County Jail/Women's Side

Mary had many piercings on her face and lip and cultic tattoos of an owl and dream catchers. She was sexually abused by her stepfather, was a weed smoker and involved in a fornicating relationship with her boyfriend.

As I begin to pray for her, she really began manifesting when I called out the abuse spirit that came by her stepfather. She told me she felt heat on her head and that her tattoos started hurting, and then she felt a release of demonic energy come out of her tattoos. She felt spirits move out of her legs from the dream catcher tattoos, also tingling in her toes. Her stomach, chest and throat cramped up as a spirit gripped her tightly, however it's power was quickly broken by the name of Yeshua.

I cast out the spirit in her back that was calling her and causing tormenting pain, in Yeshua's name and she was instantly healed. She asked in surprise, "will it stay this way?" She was taking pain medication three times a day, three discs were damaged, and now they were healed. She kept stating, 'this is weird, as she felt the spirits moving out of her in Yeshua's name. She conveyed that she had a lot of joy and felt much lighter after the deliverance through Christ's name.

DEMON MENTALITY EXPOSED

A Journal Of A Demon Deliverance Minister

Receiving The Holy Spirit

Before you enter into spiritual warfare, it is paramount that you be filled with the Holy Spirit. Jesus instructed his disciples not to leave Jerusalem until they were filled. The Savior himself did not begin His ministry until He had received the Holy Spirit at the time He was baptized by John the Baptist. He was 30 years old at the time; scripture documents that Jesus' ministry was only three years here on Earth. So, if Jesus did not start His ministry until he had received the Holy Spirit, what would make one believe that they wouldn't need to?

Acts 1:8 tells us that we will obtain power when we receive the Holy Spirit. On the streets they have a saying…"You don't take a butter knife to a gunfight. Going up against a demonic, supernatural spiritual being in the natural state, is basically like doing the same thing.

God's Word tells us that the Holy Spirit is the comforter. The Holy Spirit is an actual person with a mind, emotions and will. The Holy Spirit is the third person of the trinity, Godhead. Jesus said the Holy Spirit would bring things to our remembrance of what He had already told us. He goes on to say the Holy Spirit will not speak of His own, but His mission is always to do the perfect will of the Father as it is Christ's desire to do the same. This is why I emphasize that we are praying going into spiritual warfare, we cannot speak from our head, but only from our spirit, which, as a Believer, is directed by the Holy Spirit. This was Yeshua's methodology, our Savior states:

He that rejecteth me, and receiveth not my words, hath one that judgeth him: the word that I have spoken, the same shall judge him in the last day. For I have not spoken of myself; but the Father which sent me, he gave me a commandment, what I should say, and what

DEMON MENTALITY EXPOSED

A Journal Of A Demon Deliverance Minister

I should speak. And I know that his commandment is life everlasting: whatsoever I speak therefore, even as the Father said unto me, so I speak.

John 12:48-50

Yeshua is telling us that He only would say what His Heavenly Father would tell Him to say, and that was through the Holy Spirit. Now don't get the misconception that Jesus was just the Father's puppet, no, Yeshua has His own mind, emotions and will, however He was on a divine assignment. He willingly submitted to His Father who He was one with (1 John 5:6), to be His Father's perfect ambassador to the world. Yeshua understood that when you speak from God's spirit, which is the Holy Spirit, there is no higher power and strength than that in all the universes.

God's Word tells us that the Holy Spirit won't only just empower us, but it will also lead and guide us where to go and what to say with His anointing and boldness.

When doing the deliverance, the Holy Spirit will give you an utterance to say words not only in your heavenly language but also in your native language as you not only pray, but as you speak. God's Word tells us in John 7:38: "out of your belly shall flow rivers of living water." My utterance will be strong as I'm praying the deliverance prayer as addressing the demons within the person, a Word of Knowledge might come about the person and sometimes God will compel me what He wants me to tell them.

The Bible tells us that after we have received the Holy Spirit, that our body becomes God's official temple on the Holy Spirit.

DEMON MENTALITY EXPOSED

A Journal Of A Demon Deliverance Minister

What? know ye not that your body is the temple of the Holy Ghost which is in you, which ye have of God, and ye are not your own?

1 Corinthians 6:19

Praying in tongues through the Holy Spirit not only strengthens our spirit man, but it prays the perfect prayer to our Heavenly Father. *Romans 8:26* tells us:

Likewise the Spirit also helpeth our infirmities: for we know not what we should pray for as we ought: but the Spirit itself maketh intercession for us with groanings which cannot be uttered.

What I do in prayer, more specific, in intercessory prayer, is go before God and just mention an individual's name and then proceed to pray in tongues as I supernaturally receive an utterance from my belly. Initially there will usually be a strong utterance, I know to move on to the next person or situation to be prayed for after the utterance starts slowing down, and then comes to a stop. I'm assured at that point that I have prayed the perfect prayer, according to the perfect will of our Heavenly Father.

DEMON MENTALITY EXPOSED

A Journal Of A Demon Deliverance Minister

Prayer

Father, I come to you in humbleness reverence and gratitude to ask you by faith to receive your gift of your precious Holy Spirit and the gift of tongues, which is my heavenly language. If there is anything that would hinder me from receiving your gift, please reveal it to me now. I repent for all my sins and forgive all those who have offended me.

I also ask, Father, that when it is your will and timing that you open up my spirit's five senses, being vision, smell, touch, taste, and sound so that I may be more in tune to your will for my life.

Acts 1:8 states that I shall receive power when I receive the Holy Spirit and that out of my belly shall flow rivers of living water(*John 7:38*). By faith I receive it now in the name of Your Son Yeshua Hamashia.

*After you have prayed this prayer in faith, now be still and by faith sense the influx of the Holy Spirit and prepare to open your mouth to utter out the breath of the Holy Spirit from your belly. Remember John 7:38 tells us: "out of your belly shall flow rivers of living water."

DEMON MENTALITY EXPOSED

A Journal Of A Demon Deliverance Minister

—— PERSONAL TESTIMONY ——

Phone Deliverance

I would like to share a testimony on receiving prayer for my son. Prior to receiving prayer, when I gave birth to my son, Donald, when he was only six weeks (old) his face changed, into a very demonic face; it scared me so bad. His face then changed again when he was eight weeks in a restaurant. My friend Portia witnessed it, and she said, "Shonta did you see that? I said, yes I saw it.

I wasn't all the way right with God, and I lacked a lot of wisdom back then. When my son was six years old he did something very horrible, he was acting as if he was interested in other boys and I was crying to have learned this, so I told him, "Donald, I will pray for you, and he gave me an evil look and in a voice that wasn't his, said, "It won't work." It was the voice of a demon. I then prayed over him, and I rebuked that demon in Jesus' name. So I went to different churches to have my son prayed over, some of the people that I thought were women of God looked at me strange when I told them why my son needed prayer. None of them called me back. I then felt embarrassed to have revealed this to them about Donald.

These women of God made me feel ashamed. So Donald is 13 and he had anger issues, he has even threatened to kill himself. So, this is when I found Rayford and I received prayer for not only myself, but for Donald, While Ray was praying, Donald walked away at first, but Ray continued to pray for him. As Ray was praying, my door flew open, it scared me and Donald started feeling sick in his stomach, and when Ray finished, Donald

DEMON MENTALITY EXPOSED

A Journal Of A Demon Deliverance Minister

went in the bathroom and had to vomit. He was sick all night; he woke me up at 1:00 a.m. and said he is still sick and vomiting, and I gave him ginger ale and Pepto Bismol. He then woke up at 6:00 a.m., which is the time he wakes for school, he was still very sick. I knew this was normal when a person is prayed over so he stayed home in bed all day.

Well the good news— now it's been over a week, Donald is so full of joy, he laughs all the time. He prays and reads his Bible. He keeps his Bible in the room with him. Ray, he said to tell you 'thank you,' and he is sorry for giving you a hard time. He even threw all of his video games away. I was proud of him. He told me knew Jesus wanted him in his life, because Jesus appeared to Donald; Jesus manifested himself to my son when he was 11, and Jesus reached his hand out to my son; Donald said he had a hole in his hand. He said Jesus was at the right hand of God, he couldn't see God's face, it was like a cloud in front of his face,

He said he saw Jesus' hair, which is dark and to his shoulders. He said he has a beard also and he had a robe on. My son said this was 1,000 times better than meeting any celebrity. He was shocked, yet happy, he woke me up to tell me all about it. He said knew Jesus had a calling on his life. Thank you, Rayford for taking the time to pray for my son. God is so faithful. I'm so glad he uses people like you to pray over his children. God bless!

—Shonta

DEMON MENTALITY EXPOSED

A Journal Of A Demon Deliverance Minister

How To Start Your Day In The Lord

In order to assure success in your day, and success does not mean you're not going to have trials and tribulations. There are doctrines that are insinuating that once we are saved, we should have joy manifesting in our emotions and our face 24 hours a day. This is not so. I have many that call me after a deliverance that convey to me that they feel heavy, that something doesn't 'feel right.'

Many believe they need another deliverance. In some cases we might need to proceed with another deliverance prayer, because deliverance can be a process, not always a one-time deliverance session. However, I find for the most part, that they are just spiritually out of shape, or that God is allowing their soul and spirit to be troubled, because He has an assignment for them. Sometimes God gets our attention through our emotions or a situation.

God can manifest not only thoughts, but emotions through us, in order to move us in the direction He has destined for us. These can be emotions of sadness, joy, and yes, even anger. That is righteous anger: We see this when Jesus overthrew the money changer tables in the synagogue, because of their corruptness.

"Be ye angry, and sin not: let not the sun go down upon your wrath:"

Ephesians 4:26

We see in scripture, where Yeshua was troubled in spirit:

When Jesus had thus said, he was troubled in spirit, and testified, and said, Verily, verily, I say unto you, that one of you shall betray

DEMON MENTALITY EXPOSED

A Journal Of A Demon Deliverance Minister

me.

John 13:21

He was not possessed with the spirit of depression or any other evil spirit, the Father troubled His spirit to alert Him to pray and act on a divine assignment. God can manifest sorrow and grief in our hearts which will compel us to go pray, visit and attend to a young widow, or an abandoned child or an inmate doing a life sentence, etc.. We are the body of Christ, God places His emotions and thoughts in our spirit, to be compelled to do the works of Christ. Remember Yeshua stated, I only say and do what my Father tells me (John 12:48-50). We are the body of Christ so we should be doing what Christ did when He was here on Earth.

However, in order to do the things of Christ, we must have the mind of Christ. If you are a Believer, scripture tells us we have the mind of Christ (1 Corinthians 2:16). However, we must develop it according to Romans 12:2: And be not conformed to this world: but be ye transformed by the renewing of your mind, that ye may prove what is that good, and acceptable, and perfect, will of God.

There is a basic routine given in His Word which will assure we walk in the Spirit daily. We are three parts; body, soul and spirit. When we obtain Salvation through Yeshua Hamashia and are Born Again, our old sinful spirit dies and we are birthed with a new, sinless spirit of incorruptible seed from God:

"Seeing ye have purified your souls in obeying the truth through the Spirit unto unfeigned love of the brethren, see that ye love one another with a pure heart fervently:

DEMON MENTALITY EXPOSED

A Journal Of A Demon Deliverance Minister

Being born again, not of corruptible seed, but of incorruptible, by the word of God, which liveth and abideth for ever."

1 Peter 1:22-23

The spirit is the component within us which influences our soul. What is our soul? It is the mind, emotions and will. So the spirit influences the soul and the soul drives and animates the body. This is why scripture tells us:

Watch and pray, that ye enter not into temptation: the spirit indeed is willing, but the flesh is weak.

Matthew 26:41

Most Christians don't have a disciplined spiritual life. It's very unstructured and undisciplined. We are taught as a society to have structured discipline in almost every area of life, such as career, business, fitness etc., however there is not a lot of talk when it comes to developing a structured spiritual life. Most individuals I encounter during counseling sessions, convey to me that they have a Bible study and prayer life based on a very loose structure and casual "feel like it" basis. I remember a pastor telling me, "Part-time Christians, can't overcome full-time devils."

Here are some great foundational scriptures to meditate on in the morning:

"I can do all things through Christ who strengthens me."

Philippine 4:13

DEMON MENTALITY EXPOSED

A Journal Of A Demon Deliverance Minister

"Not by might, nor by power, but by my spirit, saith the Lord of hosts."

Zechariah 4:6

These two scriptures help to remind us, that we are going through this day, not in our power, but God's power.

"I am the vine, ye are the branches: He that abideth in me, and I in him, the same bringeth forth much fruit: for without me ye can do nothing."

John 15:5

Remember the goal is to influence our mind with the Spirit of God. Our soul needs reprogramming, before salvation it was influenced and corrupted by the world, being bent towards sin. Our soul and body is in spiritual rehab. It's like our spirit man is the correctional officer and the soul and body are the inmates being rehabilitated, to prepare to reenter society.

Remember our spirit is perfect, not because of anything we did, it's only by God's mercy and grace that he gifted us with his spirit.

"For by grace are ye saved through faith; and that not of yourselves: it is the gift of God: Not of works, lest any man should boast."

Ephesians 2:8-9

It's because of our new spirit and the blood that covers the sin of our soul and body, that allows us to come boldly before God's throne and

DEMON MENTALITY EXPOSED

A Journal Of A Demon Deliverance Minister

have fellowship with a loving God, full of mercy and grace.

"Therefore, brothers, since we have confidence to enter the Most Holy Place by the blood of Jesus,"

Hebrews 10:19
Berean Study Bible

This regiment from the Word of God will help you formulate a spiritual discipline.   We all need to get in, and stay in, spiritual shape.

Enter into his gates with thanksgiving, and into his courts with praise: be thankful unto him, and bless his name."

Psalms 100:4

Thankfulness: The soul will often fight with the spirit on being thankful. The soul innately wants to complain, and go right to asking God for needs and desires. Remember the soul was corrupted by the influences of the world, and is in spiritual rehabilitation, with the spirit as the taskmaster. Our spirit is always in sync with the Holy Spirit, which is in sync with God the Father's will. Being thankful is not only spiritually healthy, but also mentally healthy. The mental impacts our physical well being. This is why God tells us the following in His Word:

"Finally, brethren, whatsoever things are true, whatsoever things are honest, whatsoever things are just, whatsoever things are pure, whatsoever things are lovely, whatsoever things are of good report;

DEMON MENTALITY EXPOSED

A Journal Of A Demon Deliverance Minister

if there be any virtue, and if there be any praise, think on these things."

Philippians 4:8

Believe it or not, the above scripture is the cure for depression. Depression, in a nutshell is a constant pattern or frequency of brain waves of negative or sad thoughts and beliefs. Our brain waves can create frequencies, negative or positive. Depressing thoughts create negative brain waves that inhibit the neurotransmitters in the brain, which produce the "feel good" chemicals dopamine (motivational chemical) and serotonin ("happy" chemical). When your brain stops producing these chemicals, your emotions go flat, which results in depression.

Positive and happy thoughts release the neurotransmitters of dopamine and serotonin at a healthy level, which produces a positive and happy wellbeing.

Apostle Paul stated in *Acts 26:2 "I think myself happy."* Paul had the cure for depression over 2,000 years ago. Being thankful produces positive thoughts, which produces the God-given chemicals for happiness. Practicing thankfulness can take an individual from depression to joy within minutes. Thankfulness is a healthy and Godly practice.

God's names are divine and powerful in the spirit realm as well as in the natural realm. I'm talking about the original Hebrew names:

DEMON MENTALITY EXPOSED

A Journal Of A Demon Deliverance Minister

Yahweh= God

Yeshua Hamashia= Jesus Christ

Ruach Ha Kodesh= Holy Spirit

All of these names have the AH sound, which produces the healing frequency of 528 hz (vibrations per-second). This frequency has been medically proven to heal damaged cellular structure in the body. I go more in detail on this in the segment titled The Power of Frequencies in Words. Just saying these names can make you feel better, however, to get the full divine power of these Holy names, they must be spoken from the Believer's spirit.

Many individuals I counsel initially feel they have nothing to be thankful for. Many are in juvenile hall or in jail, facing long sentences, some life sentences. However, whatever situation we may be in, this is far from the case. Below is just a thankful list to jog our memory of God's Love, mercy and grace towards us. I suggest you create a personal one:

Thankful List (Example)

My name is written in the Book of Life. I have eternal life in the most spectacular place in all of the universes.

Christ, the Son of God, suffered the most brutal death imaginable on the cross, so that I could have my sins forgiven and have eternal life in Heaven's paradise.

I have food and clean water, and this is not the case for the majority

DEMON MENTALITY EXPOSED

A Journal Of A Demon Deliverance Minister

of the people on the planet.

I'm not dead or in hell, I did not die in my sins.

He protects me and my family, when I don't even know he is protecting us.

God will never leave me or forsake me. (Hebrews 13:5)

I have my health and right mind.

This list goes on and on, when we really take the time to think of God's goodness.

Practical Steps to Walking in Thankfulness:

1. Go into a Prayer Closet/Room or go on a walk.

Before you ask anything from God, just begin to thank Him. Meditate on what you're thankful for; create your own list. Appreciate God's creation all around you: trees, flowers, animals, rivers, ocean, etc.. God's Word tells us that God made us for his pleasure.

"Thou art worthy, O Lord, to receive glory and honour and power: for thou hast created all things, and for thy pleasure they are and were created."

Revelation 4:11

DEMON MENTALITY EXPOSED

A Journal Of A Demon Deliverance Minister

2. Praise: To praise God, is to give honor of who He truly is. He is a loving, forgiving, awesome God, who is faithful, trustworthy, generous, and honest. God is full of compassion, mercy and grace. We can praise Him in song or through just our words, talking to Him or through reading psalms from our heart and other scriptures that gives God praise. Here are some examples of saints praising God in scripture:

"Bless the LORD, O my soul, And all that is within me, bless His holy name. Bless the LORD, O my soul, And forget none of His benefits; Who pardons all your iniquities, Who heals all your diseases; Who redeems your life from the pit, Who crowns you with loving kindness and compassion; Who satisfies your years with good things, So that your youth is renewed like the eagle." This begins to bring God's Glory on the seen. We always have God's presence within us. The Glory is the manifestation of His presence and power."

Psalm 103:1-5

And every creature which is in Heaven, and on the earth, and under the earth, and such as are in the sea, and all that are in them, heard I saying, blessing, and honour, and glory, and power, be unto him that sitteth upon the throne, and unto the Lamb for ever and ever.

Revelations 5:13

Praise usually has a faster upbeat tempo. Joy, gratitude and honor is expressed to God through our spirit, soul and body. As you move in the spirit, you will feel a shift to slow it down, at this point you are entering into worship.

DEMON MENTALITY EXPOSED

A Journal Of A Demon Deliverance Minister

3. Worship:

God is a Spirit: and they that worship him must worship him in spirit and in truth.

John 4:26

At the point of worship, God's Glory is manifesting, we have moved from the spiritual gate and court, to the Holy of Holies, which is His throne. Remember, scripture tells us that our body is the actual temple of the Holy Spirit.

Know ye not that ye are the temple of God, and that the Spirit of God dwelleth in you?

1 Corinthians 3:16

You might even feel lighter, because your spirit man is taking over. Scripture tells us we must worship him from our spirit, not just our mind.

"God is spirit, and those who worship Him must worship in spirit and truth."

John 4:24

By faith, when you are in the spirit, God will begin to give you an utterance to speak whether in your natural language or your spiritual tongue, or both. It will come from your belly region and not just your head region. God's Word tells us:

DEMON MENTALITY EXPOSED

A Journal Of A Demon Deliverance Minister

He that believeth on me, as the scripture hath said, out of his belly shall flow rivers of living water.

John 7:38

You might be thinking this sounds foolish, if you're not filled with the Holy Spirit and you're reading this at will.

God's Word states:

But the natural man receiveth not the things of the Spirit of God: for they are foolishness unto him: neither can he know them, because they are spiritually discerned.

1 Corinthians 2:14

So, in worship we are expressing our love to Him through our spirit, being sensitive to the utterances stirring within our belly region. The spirit can also establish our thoughts during worship as what to express verbally, sing or just meditate on. Proverbs 16:3 tells us that if we commit ourselves to God, that He will establish our thoughts. Now after we have been worshiping God from our spirit, we will feel another shift at some point, which will lead us to petition God at His Throne.

4. Petition:

Be anxious for nothing, but in everything, by prayer and petition, with thanksgiving, present your requests to God.

Philippians 4:6, Berean Study Bible

DEMON MENTALITY EXPOSED

A Journal Of A Demon Deliverance Minister

Praise and worship pleases God, it brings forth the manifestation of His Glory, which is a divine time to petition God. Praise and worship brings our spirit to the forefront, so when we petition, we are petitioning according to the perfect will of God.

When we are lead by the spirit in prayer, which is synced with the Holy Spirit, we will be lead to ask not according to our will, but God's will. When we look in scripture, we see David waiting for the manifestation of God before he went to battle.

And let it be, when thou hearest the sound of a going in the tops of the mulberry trees, that then thou shalt bestir thyself: for then shall the LORD go out before thee, to smite the host of the Philistines.

2 Samuel 5:24

The basic lesson is, don't get ahead of God, wait for the manifestation of His presence, which is His glory, before moving forward. Yeshua gave us a basic foundation on how to pray:

After this manner therefore pray ye: Our Father which art in heaven, Hallowed be thy name. Thy kingdom come, Thy will be done in earth, as it is in heaven. Give us this day our daily bread. And forgive us our debts, as we forgive our debtors. And lead us not into temptation, but deliver us from evil: For thine is the kingdom, and the power, and the glory, for ever. Amen.

Matthew 6:9-13

Yeshua instructed us to pray to God the Father in His name:

DEMON MENTALITY EXPOSED

A Journal Of A Demon Deliverance Minister

And whatsoever ye shall ask in my name, that will I do, that the Father may be glorified in the Son.

If ye shall ask any thing in my name, I will do it.

John 14:13-14

However the prerequisite is, it must be according to the Father's will, not ours. This is what many miss. This is why it is a must that we discipline ourselves to read God's Word, the Holy Bible in it's entirety. There will be many times we will not know God's perfect will. In these cases, we wait on Him, until He shows us.

And this is the confidence that we have in Him, that, if we ask any thing according to his will, he heareth us:

1 John 5:14

This is why we must pray in the spirit:

Likewise the Spirit also helpeth our infirmities: for we know not what we should pray for as we ought: but the Spirit itself maketh intercession for us with groanings which cannot be uttered.

Romans 8:26

After petitioning, it's important we go to His Word, to continue to grow our faith, by getting deeper rooted in His Word.

So then faith cometh by hearing, and hearing by the word of God.

Romans 10:17

DEMON MENTALITY EXPOSED

A Journal Of A Demon Deliverance Minister

This book of the law shall not depart out of thy mouth; but thou shalt meditate therein day and night, that thou mayest observe to do according to all that is written therein: for then thou shalt make thy way prosperous, and then thou shalt have good success.

Joshua 1:8

5. Read God's Word:

As I mentioned earlier, it's a must that Believers discipline themselves to read God's Word in it's entirety. In other words, read the whole Bible, not just the "juicy" parts. It's God's letter to His children. If you wrote a letter to your children, would you be pleased if they only read half of it?

Here is a plan that worked for me. I have read the Bible over and over for years utilizing this plan daily:

*Start at the beginning:

3 Chapters-Old Testament (place a bookmark)

3 Chapters-New Testament (place a bookmark)

1-Chapter of Psalms (place a bookmark)

1-Chapter of Proverbs (place a bookmark)

When you get to the end of each section, repeat until the rapture. After you have completed this daily discipline, go in and study different sections, take notes, use highlighters, obtain study aids, go to

DEMON MENTALITY EXPOSED

A Journal Of A Demon Deliverance Minister

Bible studies, etc..

6. Listen & Wait to Hear from God:

Proverbs 16:3
Commit thy works unto the Lord, and thy thoughts shall be established.
(Through our thoughts)

Psalm 37:4
Delight thyself also in the Lord: and he shall give thee the desires of thine heart.
(By giving us His Desires)

1 Corinthians 2:16
For who hath known the mind of the Lord, that he may instruct him? but we have the mind of Christ.

As we commit our ways to God, through prayer, He will start giving us His thoughts about the situation. Then, Psalms 37:4 tells us that God will then give us His desires. This means a desire to do something or desire not to. This is how God leads us.

We delight ourselves in the Lord by spending time with Him and obeying Him. You notice that the devil will also give desires, when individuals obey him. By practicing these first two scriptures, we will learn to walk in the mind of Christ, which is righteousness and obedience.

As we pray and seek God for His wisdom, we will begin to receive His supernatural peace, then His joy, which is our strength

DEMON MENTALITY EXPOSED

A Journal Of A Demon Deliverance Minister

(Nehemiah 8:10), followed by a strong desire and faith to act on what He has placed in our hearts.

This could be to prophecy or give a word of knowledge as the Holy Spirit gives the utterance. It might also be praying and laying hands on the sick, or casting an evil spirit out of a person or breaking off a generational curse through the blood of Yeshua.

I always ask the individual to examine their heart to see if they need to repent, renounce previous activities or organizations they had been involved in such as; witchcraft, secret societies, soul-ties, etc..

I also ask if they need to forgive someone. In my own experience in the deliverance ministry, I have learned that unrepented sin and unforgiveness are the two main spiritual legalities, that satan utilizes to block an individual's healing and deliverance.

Now once you get authorization from God, then you may place demands on the Kingdom of Darkness through rebuking, binding, and loosing, etc. in Jesus' name.

Always remember, it's God's timing not ours. Everyone wants that instant miracle, healing and deliverance, including myself, but for whatever reason, it does not always happen like that.

It appears many will wait as long as up to 48 hours, putting God on a timeclock, then after the 48 hours have expired they give up, or feel they need to do it all over again, instead of just thanking and waiting on God for His perfect timing. This is why God tells us in Proverbs 3:5 for us not to lean on our own understanding. We have to learn to wait on God.

DEMON MENTALITY EXPOSED

A Journal Of A Demon Deliverance Minister

Wait for the LORD; Be strong and let your heart take courage; Yes, wait for the LORD.

Psalm 27:14

Though this might go against some of the Word of Faith doctrine, we should never make a bold decree of prophecy and healing unless God truly moved on your spirit to do so. Many Christians get overly emotional, mistaking their emotions for God's anointing, thus speaking something out which was not God's will. The collateral damage caused by lack of discernment can be irreversible.

Again, there are no shortcuts to obtaining spiritual discernment. The key is simply spending more time with God through prayer and His Word.

Spiritual discernment is vital when engaging in spiritual warfare. You can't flight an enemy you can't detect. For example; many Christians will just absorb the thought and emotions of fear and depression, not realizing that there are actual demons deploying what scripture describes as "the fiery darts." These fiery darts are thoughts manufactured by the Kingdom of Darkness.

A seasoned spiritual fighter will discern this, and will utilize their shield of faith (Ephesians 6) to repel these fearful and depressive thoughts from the evil spirits.   So how is the shield of faith utilized?

By using the meditative process I explained earlier. Meditating on God's Word produces faith and faith cancels out fear, doubt and all negativity. Ephesians 2:2 talks about satan being the prince of the power of the air. What's in the air? Frequencies. Did you know that

DEMON MENTALITY EXPOSED

A Journal Of A Demon Deliverance Minister

when we speak, our words literally and scientifically create good and bad frequencies? Proverbs 18:21 states "Life and Death are in the power of the tongue."

I have a video podcast I did about a Japanese scientist who literally proved that life and death are in the power of the tongue in a laboratory experiment. Here is an excerpt from an article I recently wrote titled, Life & Death in the Power of the Tongue.

The power of words is often taken in a symbolic manner, old rhymes such as, "sticks and stones will hurt my bones, but words will never hurt me." Many grow up believing this, however scientific data has proven this to be very far from the truth.

Einstein said that everything is energy. That includes our words and even our thoughts, both produce electric energy. This is why a dog can sense fear in an individual, the dog feels and senses the vibrations in the voice or thoughts, of whether they are positive or negative. Dr. Matsui Enomoto placed the power of words through a scientific test, in a controlled laboratory. He wanted to demonstrate how our words impact water. Why is this relevant? Because we are made up of 72% water.

In the experiment, boiled white rice was placed in three beakers, then covered with water. The first beaker was labeled "Thank you," the second beaker was labeled "You Idiot" and the third beaker was label-less. During this 30-day experiment, the first beaker labeled "Thank you," was verbally thanked every morning. The second beaker labeled "You idiot," was told "You idiot" every morning, the last beaker with no label was ignored.

DEMON MENTALITY EXPOSED

A Journal Of A Demon Deliverance Minister

After the 30 days, the beaker that had been thanked, was producing a pleasant aroma. The beaker that had been told "You idiot," had begun to rot, turning a dark black-grey. The beaker that was ignored, began to rot in a similar fashion to the second beaker. The rice in the beaker was a representative of our body, for the purpose of demonstrating the impact water has on the body. Again our words, thoughts, music etc., carries energy, whether good or bad. There is much research proving that unforgiveness and hatred can cause sickness in the body, such as cancer. There has been a rise of cancer in our society, especially in children. Could it be due to the fact that many of the mainstream music such as in gangsta rap and heavy metal, can be producing second hand vibrations of hate which are creating cancer cells?

Again we are made up of 72% water. We should be very cognizant of what type of energy we allow to impact the water within us. Negative energy can disturb our water, causing cellular damage to our bodies. On the same note, positive energy creates and maintains healthy cells in our body, thus producing healthy bodies.

It's not only our words that create frequencies, but also our thoughts. A Christian who is an experienced and discerning spiritual fighter will act on 2 Corinthians 10:5, in which we are instructed in God's Word to cast down every thought to bring it into obedience to the mind of Christ.

You see when we become a born again Christian, we literally receive a new birth within us, which is our new birth within us, which is our new spirit, which is incorruptible, perfect and equipped with the mind of Christ. The mind of Christ is full of faith and has no fear or depression.

DEMON MENTALITY EXPOSED

A Journal Of A Demon Deliverance Minister

We are body, soul and spirit. When God gave us the spirit of Christ through His Son, our old sinful spirit died. This is what baptism represents, being buried with Christ and resurrecting with the new spirit.

You see, we are three parts. Let me explain briefly the formation and process.

In general it is the spirit that influences the soul. A Christian Believer has the spirit of Christ. God's Word tells us that an unbeliever has the spirit of sin from the Kingdom of Darkness.

Wherefore, as by one man sin entered into the world, and death by sin; and so death passed upon all men, for that all have sinned.

Romans 5:12

Whatever spirit which is within them, will influence their soul, which again is the mind, emotions and will. You see, the frequency deployed from the spirit influences the mind, which stirs the emotions; during this process, the will makes the decision to accept or reject the thought which came from the spirit.

Again these thoughts and emotions create frequencies which travel into our nervous system like wifi, which impacts the brain's neurotransmitters, causing them to release or not release the biological chemicals into the body. These chemicals cause the body's system to react in a negative or positive manner. So we see the theory "cause and effect" in action. In other words, the frequencies coming from the spirit, dictate the mind and body's performance.

DEMON MENTALITY EXPOSED

A Journal Of A Demon Deliverance Minister

For example; depression, which comes from the Kingdom of Darkness, transmits a 6.66 hz frequency, according to clinical studies.

This is an unhealthy frequency, because it enters into the nervous system into the brain, which shuts down the neurotransmitters, which release dopamine and serotonin-- the feel good chemicals-- which drive our motivation and keeps us in a balance and good mood. When the neurotransmitters of these two chemicals are out of commission it causes clinical depression. Poisonous frequencies are poison to the body.

There are a large variety of frequencies good and bad, even big corporations and the entertainment industry are utilizing the knowledge of frequencies to profit from consumers.

For example, they have the scientific knowledge that the sexual lust frequency is 33 hz. Understanding this information, they can strategically place this 33z frequency within their music or commercials, which goes undetected by the consumer, which has the potential to turn unsuspected viewers and listeners into hypnotic slaves, programming them to feel compelled to purchase useless and harmful products and services from these industries over and over.

Military bases transmit out a 13 hz frequency of fear, to repel away potential intruders. There are a multitude of frequencies for every behavior and emotion you can think of. In the world of science, they are called signatures. There is literally a menu book or recipe book to create and control human behavior going back to the U.S. government's diabolical covert operation named "Paperclip," aka MK-Ultra/Monarch. In the late 1940s the Paperclip mind-control program

DEMON MENTALITY EXPOSED

A Journal Of A Demon Deliverance Minister

was being deployed on military personnel and innocent civilians by the U.S. government against their will.

We must remember the battle first starts in the mind. *Proverb 23:7 "As a man thinketh in their heart, so is he."* It is our soul in which God gives us the freewill to choose the spirit we will allow ourselves to be influenced by. Adam and Eve had the choice to eat of the fruit of good and evil in the Garden of Eden which was forbidden by God. They chose to disobey God, thus curses and death entered into the world which we are still fighting today.

When individuals choose to live a life of sin, it opens the doors for demons to come in and bring curses, sickness and death. This is why we not only need salvation, but deliverance. You see, salvation by the blood of Jesus rescues us out of satan's Kingdom of Darkness into the Kingdom of Heaven. However, many P.O.W.'s who are rescued still have the chains of addiction and sickness on them. The ministry of deliverance through the power of the Holy Spirit breaks the chains off and expels the tormentors, which are the demons.

Scripture tells us not to neglect the gifts of the Holy Spirit (1 Timothy 4:14-16, 1 Corinthians 12:1-31). These gifts such as prophecy, word of knowledge, healing, miracles, counseling, discernment of spirits, working of miracles were given to us by our Heavenly Father, through our Lord and Savior Jesus Christ to help us gain victory over the many battles we have and will have against the kingdom of darkness.

He that committeth sin is of the devil; for the devil sinneth from the beginning. For this purpose the Son of God was manifested, that he might destroy the works of the devil.

1 John 3:8

DEMON MENTALITY EXPOSED

A Journal Of A Demon Deliverance Minister

One of satan's greatest strategies was to convince the majority of Christian churches not to accept these gifts, by convincing them with various lies such as; the ministry gifts stopped with Jesus' disciples. When scripture tells us the following:

Mark 16:17-18

17 And these signs will accompany those who believe: in my name they will cast out demons; they will speak in new tongues; 18 they will pick up serpents with their hands; and if they drink any deadly poison, it will not hurt them; they will lay their hands on the sick, and they will recover."

John 14:12

12 Verily, verily, I say unto you, He that believeth on me, the works that I do shall he do also; and greater works than these shall he do; because I go unto my Father.

Hosea 4:6 says "My people perish for a lack of knowledge." In Proverbs 4:7, it tells us, *In all thy getting, get an understanding.* This is the reason why the Holy Spirit compelled me to write this message.

We must be bold as lions (Proverbs 28:1) and endure hardship like a good soldier (2 Timothy 2:3). We must fight the good fight of faith (1 Timothy 6:12). We can't just stand there and ball up when the enemy comes with these thought frequencies. We must fight back in the name of the Lord, for not only ourselves, but our families and neighbors, and yes, even our enemies!!!

DEMON MENTALITY EXPOSED

A Journal Of A Demon Deliverance Minister

7. Share Your Faith:

And he said unto them, Go ye into all the world, and preach the gospel to every creature.

Mark 16:15

*Be lead to repeat any of these steps throughout the day as the Holy Spirit prompts you.

Notes:

DEMON MENTALITY EXPOSED

A Journal Of A Demon Deliverance Minister

TESTIMONIAL STORIES

"My Personal Encounter with the Demon Of Sasha Fierce." How Demons Scientifically Utilize Musical Frequencies To Enter The Human Soul

By Evangelist Rayford Johnson-Demon Deliverance Minister

Recently Beyoncé, aka "Queen Bee," introduced the media-world and her fans to her alter-ego, Sasha Fierce. The news went viral and so did her album titled, "Sasha Fierce." Beyoncé described Sasha Fierce as a spiritual entity which comes over her and enters into her, just before she performs. The following is Beyonce in her own words...

"I have out-of-body experiences. If I cut my leg, if I fall, I don't even feel it. I'm so fearless, I'm not aware of my face or my body."

"I have someone else that takes over when it's time for me to work, and when I'm on stage, this alter ego I created that kind of protects me and who I really am. Sasha Fierce is the fun, more sensual, more aggressive, more outspoken and more glamorous side that comes out when I'm working and when I'm on the stage.'

Sasha Fierce usually appears right before Beyoncé is about to take the stage. "Usually when I hear the chords, when I put on my stilettos. Like the moment right before when you're nervous," she says. "Then Sasha Fierce appears, and my posture and the way I speak and everything is different."

DEMON MENTALITY EXPOSED

A Journal Of A Demon Deliverance Minister

"Right before I performed for the BET awards, I raised my hands up and it was the first time I felt something else come into me. I knew that was going to be my coming out night at the award show," explained Beyoncé in a recent interview.

Again, Beyoncé states "I raised my hands up and it was the first time I felt something else come into me."

When an entity enters into a person and changes their persona, this is clearly demon possession.

Note:http://beyoncetosashafierce.weebly.com/spirituality.html

Note:http://counterculturemom.com/beyonce-says-shes-demon-possessed-i-agree/

Let's now look at the name Sasha Fierce. In the spirit world, names are very important both in the Kingdom of God and the Kingdom of satan, because they carry with it an assignment. Sasha is a Russian name, meaning "defender of mankind." It's a unisex name, meaning it's both masculine and feminine. In the Luciferian religion they have a different take of Lucifer (satan).

They believe he was the "defender of mankind." In Lucefiriansism, the belief is that the God of the Holy Bible is a sadistic and stubborn deity, who keeps Adam and Eve in enslavement in the Garden of Eden. Lucifer, who shape-shifted into a serpent, became their savior by offering them freedom through the enlightenment of secret knowledge. Today this secret knowledge is known to humanity in various names such as sorcery, witchcraft, divination, black magic etc..

DEMON MENTALITY EXPOSED

A Journal Of A Demon Deliverance Minister

The Freemasons who align their doctrine with Luciferianism's also subscribe to this belief that Lucifer is the "defender of mankind." Albert Pike, one of the most notable and respected Freemasons and author of Freemasons most read and celebrated book, Morals and Dogma of the Ancient and Accepted Scottish Rite of Freemasonry, states:

"Lucifer, the Light-bearer! Strange and mysterious name to give to the Spirit of Darkness! Lucifer, the Son of the Morning! Is it he who bears the Light, and with its splendors intolerable, blinds feeble, sensual, or selfish sou*ls? Doubt it not!"* [Albert Pike, Morals and Dogma of the Ancient and Accepted Scottish Rite of Freemasonry, p. 321, 19th Degree of Grand Pontiff; Red Emphasis added]

Albert Pike is saying that Lucifer is the One who bears the Light of Freemasonry! Lucifer is the Light-bearer of Freemasonry. To those who are students of the Holy Bible, this should be of no surprise, because scripture tells us that satan can transform himself into an angel of light, 2 Corinthians 11:14.

Sasha Fierce is an antichrist spirit, her representation of her allegiance to satan is blatant in her music videos and stage performances. Symbolism in her costumes, background, along with her hand signs of the all seeing eye, pyramid, baphomet and 666 are embedded in the theme of her music. These symbols are witchcraft, for the purpose of spell bounding her audience to be subconsciously programmed with satanic/New World Order (NWO) doctrine and values. For more information on how symbols are utilized in witchcraft for mind control, please watch ThugExposed.Org's podcast titled T.V. Mind Control/Sigil Magick and The Powerful Influence of Music. You can watch them at www.thugexposed.org

DEMON MENTALITY EXPOSED

A Journal Of A Demon Deliverance Minister

Definition of fierce

(Full-Definition)

fiercer   fiercest

1

a : violently hostile or aggressive in temperament

b : given to fighting or killing : pugnacious

2 a : marked by unrestrained zeal or vehemence ‹a fierce argument›

b : extremely vexatious, disappointing, or intense ‹fierce pain›

3: furiously active or determined ‹make a fierce effort›

4: wild or menacing in appearance

fierceness noun

*Note: http://www.merriam-webster.com/dictionary/fierce

Now let's look at the second part of her name, Fierce. As we can see in the above definition of the word, "fierce" aligns with many of the attributes of the Kingdom of Darkness— violently hostile or aggressive in temperament, given to fighting or killing.

DEMON MENTALITY EXPOSED

A Journal Of A Demon Deliverance Minister

These are clearly not the fruits of the spirit of God as described in Galatians 5:22.

The fruit of the Spirit is love, joy, peace, long suffering, gentleness, goodness, and faith. Sasha Fierce's character clearly displays the fruits of the flesh as described in Galatians 5:19-21:

19 Now the works of the flesh are manifest, which are these: adultery, fornication, uncleanness, lasciviousness,

20 idolatry, witchcraft, hatred, variance, emulations, wrath, strife, seditions, heresies,

21 Envyings, murders, drunkenness, revellings, and such like: of the which I tell you before, as I have also told you in time past, that they which do such things shall not inherit the Kingdom of God.

This is why the NWO, aka Illumanati, is using the demons of Sasha Fierce to stir up a race war. The world saw this message clearly displayed at her 2016 Super Bowl performance, as she and her ackground dancers were dressed up in black militant attire as she marched out as Sasha Fierce singing her song, Formation. I'm not going into details behind the deception of the Black lives matter movement, other than to say it was funded by New World Order globalist and billionaire George Soros. Soros invested $33 million of his own money to start the Black Lives Matter movement, 33 is a magical number of numerology for the Masonic order. The mission or end game of the race war strategy is to create a police state, with 24-hour surveillance and transparency of all global citizens. By creating extreme chaos, citizens will plead for order, at any cost... which is the Illuminati/ Masonic creed, which is "order out of chaos."

DEMON MENTALITY EXPOSED

A Journal Of A Demon Deliverance Minister

In a nutshell, if you create enough fear through chaos, it is easy to legislate a police surveillance state, thus we have the Patriot Act, which undermines the U.S. Bill of Rights, which was instituted to protect our rights. The Second Amendment of the Bill of Rights gives U.S. citizens the right to bear arms. You see, the real motive behind political gun control is not to protect citizens, but to ensure that there will be little to no resistance, when Martial law and the NWO move into take full-control for the antichrist.

Sasha Fierce's agenda is to condition the masses of humanity to embrace the antichrist's satanic and socialist agenda. The Illuminati's selection of government is communism, which basically is socialism. They say communism is just socialism in a hurry. Best description on this would be an Orwellian society, often described as "big brother." Let's look at the Merriam-Webster Dictionary's definition of communism:

communism:

noun com·mu·nism \?käm-y?-?ni-z?m, -yü-

a way of organizing a society in which the government owns the things that are used to make and transport products (such as land, oil, factories, ships, etc.) and there is no privately owned property

Full Definition of COMMUNISM

1 a : a theory advocating elimination of private property

b : a system in which goods are owned in common and are available to all as needed

DEMON MENTALITY EXPOSED

A Journal Of A Demon Deliverance Minister

2

capitalized

a : a doctrine based on revolutionary Marxian socialism and Marxism-Leninism that was the official ideology of the Union of Soviet Socialist Republics

b : a totalitarian system of government in which a single authoritarian party controls state-owned means of production

c : a final stage of society in Marxist theory in which the state has withered away and economic goods are distributed equitably

d : communist systems collectively

http://www.merriam-webster.com/dictionary/communism

So basically the government takes, manages and controls every aspect of it's citizens. Meaning a totalitarian system, where the citizens have no right to private property. This is in perfect harmony with the blueprint of the New World Order. The antichrist will have nothing less than a totalitarian system of government.

* Note:http://www.behindthename.com/name/sasha

In short, Sasha Fierce represents; hedonism, rebellion, sexual lust, fornication, adultery, rage, violence, socialism, and satanism-- the same Babylonian-Jezebel spirit which opposes God in the Book of Revelation.

DEMON MENTALITY EXPOSED

A Journal Of A Demon Deliverance Minister

Notwithstanding, I have a few things against thee, because thou sufferest that woman Jezebel, which calleth herself a prophetess, to teach and to seduce my servants to commit fornication, and to eat things sacrificed unto idols.

Revelation 2:20

1 And there came one of the seven angels which had the seven vials, and talked with me, saying unto me, Come hither; I will shew unto thee the judgment of the great whore that sitteth upon many waters:

2 With whom the kings of the earth have committed fornication, and the inhabitants of the earth have been made drunk with the wine of her fornication.

3 So he carried me away in the spirit into the wilderness: and I saw a woman sit upon a scarlet coloured beast, full of names of blasphemy, having seven heads and ten horns.

4 And the woman was arrayed in purple and scarlet colour, and decked with gold and precious stones and pearls, having a golden cup in her hand full of abominations and filthiness of her fornication:

5 And upon her forehead was a name written, Mystery, Babylon The Great, The Mother Of Harlots And Abominations Of The Earth.

6 And I saw the woman drunken with the blood of the saints, and with the blood of the martyrs of Jesus:

DEMON MENTALITY EXPOSED

A Journal Of A Demon Deliverance Minister

and when I saw her, I wondered with great admiration.

7 And the angel said unto me, Wherefore didst thou marvel? I will tell thee the mystery of the woman, and of the beast that carrieth her, which hath the seven heads and ten horns.

Revelation 17:1-7

This is the spirit that satan wants to deploy into the souls of young girls and women and even the males of this generation. The Sasha Fierce mentality is just one of the foundational mind-sets for satan's New World Order, to be led by the coming antichrist, according to God's Word, the Holy Bible.

As a Christian demon deliverance minister, I have encountered many demons within individuals which came in through sinful secular music. Demons are not biased in the genre of music they will utilize. Just a note... satanic music is not just heavy metal and gangsta rap, it's any music which has a message that opposes God's Word, the Holy Bible.

I have expelled demons out of R&B, heavy metal & rap recording artists and their fans, by the Name of Yeshua Hamashia (Hebrew for Jesus Christ).

17 And these signs shall follow them that believe; In my name shall they cast out devils; they shall speak with new tongues;

Mark 16:17

DEMON MENTALITY EXPOSED

A Journal Of A Demon Deliverance Minister

During these demonic manifestations, eyes have rolled back to where there were no pupils, growling, coughing and violent posturing would occur. Demons manifest in a variety of paranormal ways. During these deliverances many have testified that they felt things moving around in their body; many say it felt like snakes were inside of them. Some have reported fiery, burning sensations (When I had called for the fire of the Holy Spirit in Yeshua's Name). The majority also report feeling physically lighter, with a much clearer mind.

In some sessions I have had the demon(s) manifest in the individual and literally speak out through the individual's mouth in anger and at times fear. On occasions these demons have attempted to negotiate with me, in order to stay in the individual.

Such was the case with my encounter with the demons of Sasha Fierce. Yes, I said demons of Sasha Fierce. There are legions of them which go by the name of Sasha Fierce. I have had three recent theatrical episodes with these demons. The first was an R&B recording artist out of Chicago, who contacted me through my website. She reported to me she was having paranormal experiences of demons jumping on her when she would lie down and even molesting her. This torment would go on night after night.

As I begun to call out the demonic spirits by name, as the Holy Spirit gave me word of knowledge, the demons started to manifest through her, she began to scream, growl, cough and vomit as the demons were being expelled out of her. At one point during the deliverance, the Holy Spirit gave me a word of knowledge to call out the demon of Sasha Fierce. I at first questioned it, as doubt crept in, thinking this was coming from my imagination. It seemed odd to my natural mind, however I felt compelled by my spirit to proceed.

DEMON MENTALITY EXPOSED

A Journal Of A Demon Deliverance Minister

At which point I said, "Demon of Sasha Fierce, manifest in the name of Yeshua Hamashia and every spirit under your command!" After a fierce growl which came out of the woman, the demon yelled out through the very petite R&B recording artist, "She's mine, she's mine, you can't have her!" This demon was very vocal and defiant, refusing to come out without a fight. The resistance of this demon broke after a couple of minutes, then it came out with an eery and loud scream.

My next encounter was with a former fashion model from Washington D.C., who had contacted me through my website, requesting prayer for marijuana addiction, anger, suicidal thoughts, depression, voices in the head and lust. As I started praying for her over the phone, demons began to manifest within a couple of minutes, through coughing and growling. Again the Holy Spirit prompted me to call out the demon of Sasha Fierce. This petite woman begin to growl and scream, then abruptly, the demon spoke out through her in a deep, manly and beastly voice, "You can't have her, you can't have her, she's mine," followed by bunch of angry rambling, which I couldn't make out. Again the demon resisted violently, then came out with a boisterous scream. After the expulsion, the young woman began weeping uncontrollably in relief and joy.

It is important to note, that both of these African American women were fans of Beyoncé and her album Sasha Fierce and both proclaimed to be Christians.

My last and most recent encounter with the demon Sasha Fierce was with a Caucasian woman, who was a hair stylist living in Missouri. She contacted me through my 1-800 prayer number asking for prayer to break a soul-tie from her deceased boyfriend.

DEMON MENTALITY EXPOSED

A Journal Of A Demon Deliverance Minister

She also requested prayer for a heroin addiction, tormenting voices in her head, suicidal thoughts, depression, meth addiction and lust. She then later added, that she was being sexually molested by demons at night. This spirit which comes to torment, molest and even rape women, is known as an Incubus demon.

The deliverance went similar to the others, a quick manifestation of demons, however when I was led by the Holy Spirit to call out the spirit of Sasha Fierce, this demon became more violent and vocal than the previous ones. It literally sounded like a huge demonic beast, speaking out of this woman. There was no hint of a female tone in the voice. It sounded like a WWF wrestler growling and yelling at their intimidated opponent. This demon took almost five minutes to lose resistance and like the others, it came out with a roaring scream, followed by the woman weeping uncontrollably in relief and joy.

"In all thy getting get understanding."

Proverbs 4:7

Demonic spirits work in tandem with scientific principles to accomplish their mission or objectives. Let me first explain how and why they work through music: Dr. Roy H. Williams, Ph.D, author of the book, Thought Particles, has a company which conducts seminars to businesses on how to create successful advertisements, which influences the subconscious part of the brain to draw people to their product or service.

Dr. Williams presents the brain in two parts: the left-brain, as the skeptic which is our conscious state, the part of the brain that comprehends

DEMON MENTALITY EXPOSED

A Journal Of A Demon Deliverance Minister

the words you are reading right now. Our right side, which is our subconscious, records everything we hear and see, even if we are unaware, this goes on 24 hours a day. It's like a 24-hour audio and video recorder.

He talks about the powerful effects of music. He states that music has the power to bypass the left hemisphere of the brain, which is our skeptic, and go directly into the right hemisphere of the brain. Later during the sleep cycle, the right brain (subconscious mind) transfers the message back to the left brain, which then influences the beliefs and behaviors of the individual, unknowingly.

For example, a person says they listen to a "gangsta rap" song just for the beat, though they believe they are blocking the message consciously with their left brain, their right brain is recording everything, even any backward masked messages.

Our right side is so intelligent, that it will take the message and transfer it back to our left-brain without us even knowing it, which will then influence our beliefs, emotions and behaviors.

How Demons Use Music To Enter The Human Soul

Practitioners of witchcraft, which includes the new age movement, understand that everything created on earth and within the universe has a frequency, or vibration. Believe it or not, our words, feelings, smell, taste, touch, emotions and even our thoughts register an electric frequency. Even before science textbooks, the occult had long before gathered this information from the Ancient Egyptian Book of the Dead, which is known in cult circles as the mother of all witchcraft books, which I explain in my

DEMON MENTALITY EXPOSED

A Journal Of A Demon Deliverance Minister

video podcast titled, T.V. Mind Control-Sigil Magick.

Did you know that depression has been proven clinically to have a 6.66 hz (vibrations per-second) frequency. How demonic is that? 6.66. I think it's interesting that the Holy Bible says in Nehemiah 8:10, that the "Joy of Lord is our strength." Now the opposite of joy is depression, and it's frequency just happens to be the same number as the antichrist, aka "Mark of the Beast." Satan is anti-God, and depression is anti-joy.

Love and happiness registers at approximately 528 hz frequency, and sexual lust has a 33 hz frequency, often conjured up by a deep bass drum. A study was conducted by sex researchers in Daytona Beach in the mid 1990s, it was called Project Q. (I'll share a link on the subject, http://www.davidjayjordan.com/33HertzandSex.html.)

Satan knows sex sells and so does the entertainment industry, so it is no surprise why R&B and rap music utilizes the deep-bass beats, in tandem with scantily clothed dancers and models in highly sexual themed music videos. Sasha Fierce's character and music is saturated in frequencies of lust, anger, violence, and an antichrist theme. These demonic frequencies from the Kingdom of Satan are deployed out to inspire the multitudes of humanity to act out in sinful and depraved behaviors.

"My people perish for a lack of knowledge."

Hosea 4:6

DEMON MENTALITY EXPOSED

A Journal Of A Demon Deliverance Minister

How Musical Frequencies Impact the Human Soul & Body

When musical frequencies enter the human nervous system (which is electric), they have been pre-encoded with information, which is then transmitted to the neurotransmitters in the brain, which then release chemicals to the body to respond to the frequency's content or program. The soul and body may respond in a positive way or negatively, all depending on the type of frequencies which have entered. God's Word tells us that "Life and death are in the power of the tongue." Proverbs 18:21. Our words and thoughts carry a frequency, all of them. This is why it is wise to watch what we say and what we think. Proverbs 23:7 states, "As a man thinketh so is he."

Dr. Caroline Leaf, a cognitive neuroscientist with a PhD in Communication Pathology, specializing in Neuropsychology states, "You are what you think: 75-98% of mental and physical illnesses come from our thought life!"

Note:* http://drleaf.com/blog/you-are-what-you-think-75-98-of-mental-and-physical-illnesses-come-from-our-thought-life/

It is vital to understand that our words, and even our thoughts, can cause our body and the bodies of others, to react in a healthy way or an unhealthy way. When we allow and create positive frequencies, our body is at peace and at ease. When we allow and create negative frequencies, are body is at dis-ease, thus the word disease.

In a nutshell, these frequencies act in the same way as computer software. The frequency being the software program and the body and soul being the computer hardware. There are only two software engineer com-

DEMON MENTALITY EXPOSED

A Journal Of A Demon Deliverance Minister

panies in the spirit world creating software to download into humanity, and that is the Kingdom of God and the Kingdom of Satan. We all create spiritual software through our words, talents and actions. The question is, what spiritual software company are you working for?

The Kingdom of Satan's software causes viruses of immoral thoughts and values, which leads to curses, bad health and eventually death. The Kingdom of God's software, is Holy and Righteousness which brings forth wisdom, blessings and eternal-life.

"The wages of sin is death."

Romans 6:23

" I came to bring life and life more abundantly."

John 10:10

Like Norton's virus protector to the home computer, we all need a virus protector to protect us from the harmful frequencies swimming around in this world system. Only through Jesus Christ can we obtain a free subscription of the divine virus protection, which is bundled with God's perfect love and peace.

For the weapons of our warfare are not carnal, but mighty through God to the pulling down of strongholds;

2 Corinthians 10:4

Who hath delivered us from the power of darkness, and hath translated us

DEMON MENTALITY EXPOSED

A Journal Of A Demon Deliverance Minister

into the kingdom of his dear Son:

Colossians 1:10-14

Casting down imaginations, and every high thing that exalteth itself against the knowledge of God, and bringing into captivity every thought to the obedience of Christ;

2 Corinthians 10:5

For who hath known the mind of the Lord, that he may instruct him? But we have the mind of Christ.

1 Corinthians 2:16

If you would like to find out more about obtaining a relationship with Yeshua Hamashia's (Jesus Christ in Hebrew) and for a Deliverance Prayer, there is a Salvation and Deliverance Prayer following.

God Bless,
Brotha Ray

DEMON MENTALITY EXPOSED

A Journal Of A Demon Deliverance Minister

R&B SINGER'S ESCAPE FROM SATANIC...."HELLYWOOD"

THE JACQUE LARUE STORY
INTERVIEW & STORY BY RAYFORD JOHNSON,
AUTHOR OF THUG MENTALITY EXPOSED

"When I was on stage something came over me. It was like nowadays, Beyonce says she has Sasha Fierce," said former R&B artist Jacque LaRue.

Jacque was a member of LaRue, a rising R&B group back in the late 1980s, discovered by producer and musical artist Jay King.

Jacque told this interviewer of her re-occurring paranormal experience.

"At the time I wasn't saved, so I didn't understand it. I got on stage; we were singing Tell Me Something Good, so I had a lead. I could sense I was not myself. Something came over me, it was almost like I went to sleep and woke up...quickly. I got on stage, I grabbed the mic and I started to go forth, and when I went forth I changed into this person.

It was a mental transition, it was an awakening, it's like you walked into one room, then you walked into another and everything was different, you knew you were different, and you kind of liked it, because you were beyond yourself. You were bolder, you weren't afraid any more. It was more than an adrenaline rush. It stayed with me through the whole concert, until I finished that song and then I sensed it dying down. It was really, really bizarre. That spirit was common for that area, for L.A., that club atmosphere."

Jacque was born and raised in Sacramento, California. She comes from a very musical background.

DEMON MENTALITY EXPOSED

A Journal Of A Demon Deliverance Minister

"I knew I would make it," she says.

She even prophesied to friends and family in her teenage years that she would be one day limo driven in New York City. This became a reality in 1987, when the group was booked for a record signing in the world famous Harlem Record Shack, a record store across the street from Harlem's famed Apollo Theatre. Their song Can't Hold On, off the Penitentiary III movie soundtrack, was steadily moving up the charts in New York City during that era.

It was at this time, God would start to open up Jacque's eyes to the true reality of Hollywood. Not a Christian at the time, Jacque described herself as a worldly, angry and mentally unstable young woman.

"I carried guns, I had a 357 magnum in my car." When this interviewer asked why, Jacque responded, *"I was just crazy, I had a lot of anger in my life, I was very angry, a lot of suppressed anger, a lot of hurt."*

Jacque had encountered numerous negative encounters with some self-proclaimed Christians during her teenage and young adult years.

"Oh, I hated them. Oh, I hated Christians. To be real, I hated them because they judged me. I was a tomboy in a sense, I loved guys, but I liked to be athletic. I was very athletic in school, at home and I just loved sports. I hated the term 'tomboy' and I always wore jeans. So I went to a couple of churches with some family friends. They were real traditional churches and when they saw me wearing pants, folks just frowned up at me. Folks wouldn't even want to talk to me. I would come up to them and be smiling, because I'm a very friendly person. I would walk up to them ready to introduce myself, and they would kind of just turn away from me, like they were better than me."

DEMON MENTALITY EXPOSED

A Journal Of A Demon Deliverance Minister

The portal of "Hellywood" would literally open up it's satanic mouth wide-open to the members of Sacramento's LaRue, with a lucrative offer of wealth and fame, soon after the record signing in Harlem. Hear it from Jacque's own words:

"I was hanging out with Tina Marie and Klymaxx, and the manager of Klymaxx was there, and a couple other actresses and actors were there. We were invited to the manager of Kymaxx's house in L.A. She had this beautiful home that was overlooking the hills, her window displayed the view of L.A., it was beautiful."

"She started talking about the sun, the moon and the stars."

This went on for some time. At a certain point during her talk, themed around sorcery and witchcraft, Jacque conveyed that the woman mysteriously paused, and an aura of a devilish charm was spell-bound upon her and it was as if it saturated and possessed her eyes.

"The way she looked at us, was 'like I'm inviting you, I want you to come and I want you to stay.'"

At this time Jacque said her friend (a fellow group member) and roommate who was a Christian, yet obviously not living it, saw a very evil presence on the woman. Her friend said to her, 'We are in trouble, we have to leave now.'"

Her friend, who was scared and disturbed by the encounter, started praying fervently when they got back to their apartment.

"So, we go to sleep and I wake up in the middle of the night, because I have this crazy dream." Jacque goes on to explain, "That dream was a dream of

DEMON MENTALITY EXPOSED

A Journal Of A Demon Deliverance Minister

an orgy. There were guys, girls, demons, it was beyond real. I saw the demon manifestations in the orgy. It was beyond words. I can't even describe the fear, it was real and I knew it was my future."

These things happen in Hollywood, I asked?

"All the time, all the time, it's a norm, but I was never a part of it, but I was going to, they were introducing me to it," she said. "The enemy was preparing me for that, not to mention, Satan had already spoken in my mind that I was not going to live to be 30. You couldn't convince me that it wasn't going to happen."

"We had these Christian folks come up, a Christian couple, Rodney and Felicia Willis and Deborah Willis. They arrived at our apartment at 12 midnight." They had initially came all the way from Sacramento to witness and pray for their male roommate, who was a music producer in the business. "They start praying for him and a demon manifest in him."

Jacque described that the man was growling, convulsing and vomiting. "Finally the devil comes out of him, and he was different, his demeanor was different, everything about him was different and when he got up, he looked at me differently."

"So they started getting into a circle. They said, 'Jacque, would you like prayer?' This is like the
second time Christian folks asked if I wanted prayer, and I'm thinking yeah, you're going to pray for me, then you're going to sleep with me, what?"

"I was really angry, I was depressed, I had issues." I said, 'sure, whatever,' so I got into the prayer circle, and Deborah Willis started praying. She said, ' if there is anyone here that would like to receive Christ into their life, the time is now!' And I heard a voice, and it was Jesus. He said, 'the time is now' and

DEMON MENTALITY EXPOSED

A Journal Of A Demon Deliverance Minister

he said it so sweet and so kind, and I opened my eyes and said 'It's time!' They smiled, it was my time, I was waiting for this time."

"I prayed the sinner's prayer, then they started laying hands on me and praying for me. Now what I was doing physically, I don't know," but where my spirit went, I left and I had a vision.

The first vision, I was no longer in the room with them, I went somewhere else. I felt my spirit leave my body to another dimension and it was a vision, it was a very clear vision, and I was in the middle of a street and I was watching myself getting into a vehicle. I had already made it, I saw it, I was rich, I was big time, everybody knew who I was."

Then I looked at myself, and I saw L.O.S.T. written on my forehead and I thought 'wow,' then all of a sudden, I don't know what type of transition it was, it felt like I popped into another vision and this vision was dark. Like dark, but you could touch it, it was tangible darkness, like you could move it with your fingers. It was dreadful and fear came over me, it was a fear of separation, it was a fear that I never, ever, ever want to experience again. It was hell, I knew it beyond a shadow of a doubt. If you die and go to hell, your first torment is separation from God. I said, 'Lord, please don't ever show me that vision again, I don't ever want to experience that again in my entire life.'"

"The third vision was a vision of Heaven. It was Jesus, and He was ushering me through Heaven. He showed me what looked like a sea, but it was people, it was so vast, innumerable and he said, 'These are the people you will touch, if you serve me.'

Right after Jesus spoke those words, Jacque says her spirit was immediately transported back into the apartment. "People were praying for me, it was no longer strange to me, I was one with them. I had this urgency to get back to

DEMON MENTALITY EXPOSED

A Journal Of A Demon Deliverance Minister

to Sacramento. I had a craving to get into God's Word. I had an insatiable hunger to get in God's Word. 'Go home, go home,' was just all in me. There is no description of the joy of the Lord, it's amazing."

Jacque LaRue is serving the Lord now as an evangelist and owns a gospel music label with her sisters called La Rue Records: moprayermopower@gmail.com.

How To Meditate On God's Word

As a Christian deliverance minister, I often have those whom had evils spirits of addictions, sickness etc.. casted out of them in the name of Yeshua (Jesus), call me a week or months later after their deliverance and healing, perplexed why they are being suddenly oppressed or have been taken captive by the Kingdom of Darkness again.

There could be numerous reasons why it has happened. It could be they opened the portal of their soul again through engaging in sin, which gives a spiritual legality for demons to enter. This happens by harboring unforgiveness or plainly they allowed satan's demons to relentlessly bully them until they just balled up in defeat.

The majority of the time, the refusal to fight-back through the power of Christ is the case. You see, after one receives deliverance and healing from Jesus, the war does not end, it often intensifies. After

DEMON MENTALITY EXPOSED

A Journal Of A Demon Deliverance Minister

they are delivered from the enemy's camp, many Christians still go through life with a victim mentality. They go to church with a victim mentality, hoping for others to fight the devil for them, not with them. Most of them have never been trained to fight a spiritual battle. They go to churches where the pastors feed the congregations just spiritual milk like kittens, never receiving the meat they will need to grow up to become lions. Demons are not afraid of kittens.

When these individuals get attacked with a thought or fiery dart, instead of deflecting it with the shield of faith and attacking back with the sword of the spirit, which is the Word of God, they just absorb the demons blows like a pen cushion. The problem here is that they don't understand the powerful authority they have in Christ. It's kind of like a correctional officer going into a prison, looking and acting very timid, giving instructions to the hardcore inmate population in a very low and fearful voice. Working in corrections for over 13 years, I will be the first to tell you, the officer that behaves this way, will have no respect or cooperation among the majority of the inmate population. Many Christians act like that correctional officer when faced against the Kingdom of Darkness.

They will share with me the extreme tormenting thoughts and emotions they are experiencing, such as depression, fear, substance abuse temptation, anger, anxiety, lust, etc.. Some say the demons will talk to them in an audible voice all night and even throughout the day. After listening, I then will ask, "While this was happening, what did you do? This question is usually followed by a long duration of silence. Almost as if they are surprised that I even asked the question.

I remind them of Ephesians 6:12, that we are in a spiritual war and

DEMON MENTALITY EXPOSED

A Journal Of A Demon Deliverance Minister

that God's Word tells us to endure hardship like a good soldier (2 Timothy 2:3).

Would you allow someone off the street to point their finger repeatedly at your forehead and call you names and speak negatively about every area of your life, including your family? Would you just stand there and say "ouch!" and then ball up on the ground and cry? Would you agree that anyone who would would act in this fashion would be easy prey for bullies and thieves?

While the victim is on the ground, they could rob them for all they have, they could even follow them home and even rob their house. It would be an easy crime job, why? Because you have a victim that won't fight back.

When a Christian can't fight well spiritually or refuses to fight at all, word gets around through the demonic network. Demons love to gang up on easy prey.

DEMON MENTALITY EXPOSED

A Journal Of A Demon Deliverance Minister

--- **PERSONAL TESTIMONIAL** ---

Phone Deliverance

"I contacted Brotha Ray for prayer and advice regarding why my asthma never seemed to be going away, getting healed or delivered. I am familiar with the deliverance and healing ministry and have been through a lot of it, but could not seem to shake the 'unshakable' spirit that was causing my lungs to tighten and shorten my breath. I would lose hours of sleep every night due to lack of breath due to battling the Spirit. But the spirit knew something I did not and would not leave.

So when on the phone with Bro Ray, he asked me if I had any unforgiveness or unrepentant sins. I assured him I did not, but gave him the down low on what traumatic events had previously taken place in my life. He also asked me if I heard voices. I told him I do hear voices when I try to sleep, mostly the voice is calling my name and tries to hold conversations with me. I also see orbs and have many spiritual dreams and manifestations at night time regarding sleep paralysis, which entered through my mother's side of the family via witchcraft.

Brotha Ray prayed for me, via phone call and as soon as he said the words, "Holy Ghost Fire" my face got extremely hot, and my head began to hurt. My right ear began to sting. He kept repeating the words and I could feel things move around in my chest, feet, hip, pelvis, and brain area. After persistent commands to the demons to come out, I began to cough and cough, until I threw up. Right after I threw up, it was followed with a sneeze. Praise the Lord Jesus Christ that He would have the Mercy and Grace to shed His Blood to have me healed and delivered."

Joshua – Prayer report

DEMON MENTALITY EXPOSED

A Journal Of A Demon Deliverance Minister

Deliverance Of The Antichrist Spirit

I waited a while before anyone entered through the door of the Juvenile Hall Bible study. The Raiders and the Chiefs were playing Thursday night football and most of the wards were glued to the television in the unit's recreational center. I had said a prayer on my way down the hallway to the unit, petitioning God to draw those individuals he wanted into the Bible study.

After about 10 minutes, three African-American wards enter. Two were regular attendees, both of whom Yeshua had delivered from hearing voices in their heads, drugs, insomnia, and gangs among other spirits.

A new ward, who I had not met walks in boldly with an intense look on his face and has a seat. Then quickly gets back up and says "Do you mind if I sit over here next to you." I say, "No problem."

During the Bible study I begin to tell them about a testimony of a deliverance at the County Jail of a gangsta rap music producer. I share that this individual started manifesting a demon violently. His eyes rolled back to where all you could see was the whites of his eyes, he began breathing in a beastly manner, clinching his seat with his hands as if he was halfway restraining himself from attacking me.

This ward became really intrigued by the story, asking a barrage of questions and wanting intricate details about the process of this individual's manifestation and deliverance.

He then conveyed to me that he believed there was an evil spirit within him.

DEMON MENTALITY EXPOSED

A Journal Of A Demon Deliverance Minister

He later told me that there have been wards at the facility that would look at him and say, "I seen the devil in you." He said they would be serious, and it happened on more than one occasion.

As the Bible study concluded, I looked over to him and asked, "Are you a Christian?" He replied, "I'm Jewish." I have to admit, that caught me off guard, in that he carried himself with the "hardcore" street thug persona and was gang affiliated. He told me from a young age he had practiced the Jewish faith in his household. So I took him for his word on it.

I then explained to him that in order to get delivered from the evil spirit, it was necessary that he have a relationship with "the Deliverer," Yeshua Hamashia. I knew through my studies that the Jewish faith denies Yeshua as Lord and Savior and does not believe he is the Son of God.

So instead of debating with the ward I said, "Is it OK that I pray and petition the throne that Yeshua shows himself real to you?" He shrugged his shoulders and nodded in agreement. I then proceeded to command the demonic spirits of witchcraft, sorcery, drugs, gangs and so on to manifest.

As I called down the fire of the Holy Spirit to burn these spirits out of their hiding place, he begins staring up at me from his head bowed in the chair as if he is paranoid about what was going on. Shortly into the prayer I felt compelled by the Lord through a word of knowledge that He gave me to address the spirit of the antichrist. In that the Jewish religion is truly and publicly antichrist.

Being lead by the Holy Spirit, I commanded "spirit of the antichrist manifest in Yeshua's name, fire of Ruach Ha Kodesh (Holy Spirit in Hebrew), burn this spirit and every spirit under the authority of this spirit out of their hiding place."

DEMON MENTALITY EXPOSED

A Journal Of A Demon Deliverance Minister

The ward immediately lifts up from his bowed position and grabs his chest with a very fearful wide-eyed look, looking at me and around the room and his peers intensely. Gasping he tells me, "My heart is beating hella fast." He then stretches over to lay over on a desk right next to him. He keeps reciting, 'my heart, it's beating fast' and tells me he feels something moving around in his chest.

He then looks at me, states in an agonizing tone, "I need to leave and get some water." I know at this point that the demon is trying to get him to leave so he can remain in him. I then ask him to hold on, and plead with him that we need to deal with this.

He stretches back in his chair still with his hand on his chest. I say, "Do you see that Jesus is real. He says, "Yes." I then ask, "Are you ready to receive Him as you Lord and Savior?" He nods in agony and saying, "yes."

I lead him into a prayer of salvation and the infilling of the Holy Spirit, knowing how we have a legal right to cast the demons out. I then commanded in prayer, "Angel of the Lord, put your sword into the chief demon in his heart region, spirit of antichrist put a chain of fire around his neck and every demon under his authority, fire of Ruach Ha Kodesh all over your spiritual bodies, I command you to go now to the pit of hell!!!"

I then begin to call out the same demons I told to manifest to also go to the pit of hell. After about five minutes of spiritual warfare he lifted his head up in relief. I asked him how he felt, he told us that he felt things moving around in his chest, going up and down from his neck to his chest. I then asked him if he felt it leave and he said,"Yes," smiling. He also stated that he felt lighter and conveyed that he also felt happy and peaceful. He kept thanking me. I told him, "Thank Jesus. He's your Deliverer."

DEMON MENTALITY EXPOSED

A Journal Of A Demon Deliverance Minister

How To Spiritually Fight

Before I pray for an individual, I always make it a point to convey to them how vital it is to learn and train for spiritual warfare.

Many who come for the deliverance and healing prayer believe the process to be like taking an aspirin or getting an oil change. Naively believing the battle is over and that they can just go back to a normal regular life. Though they will obviously be better after getting delivered and healed, the Biblical fact remains however, that we are still in a war, meaning there are future battles to come, especially after a healing or deliverance, why? Because the Kingdom of Darkness is angry that they lost their fortress, which is the body and soul. However, satan and his demons are often confident that they can retake the fort of most Christians, because the majority have not been taught or trained to do spiritual warfare with the Kingdom of Darkness.

You see, God's Word tells us to endure hardship like a good soldier.
Thou therefore endure hardness, as a good soldier of Jesus Christ. No man that warreth entangleth himself with the affairs of this life; that he may please him who hath chosen him to be a soldier.

2 Timothy 2:3-4

Proverbs 28:1 tells us that the righteous are bold as a lion. Most Christians take blow after blow from the enemy, blows of tormenting and fearful thoughts, voices, etc.. Some respond back with the Word of God for a short duration, however cave in by the end of the day. Many don't even fight at all, they just allow themselves to rest in vic-

DEMON MENTALITY EXPOSED

A Journal Of A Demon Deliverance Minister

tim mode and become a life size human pen cushion for satan and his demons.

To win these spiritual battles, it is critical that one switch from victim mentality to victor mentality. The Lord gave me this revelation as I was counseling a brother in Christ who was suffering from the spiritual victim syndrome.

I conveyed to him that he had to break free from the rabbit mentality and begin to develop a lion mentality, based on Proverbs 28:1. The scripture tells us that the righteous are bold as a lion and we have been made righteous by the blood of Jesus. As Christians we have to get on to active duty.

You see a rabbit bounces around the battlefield with high anxiety and fear, trying not to be seen or captured by the enemy. They stay in constant fear, just looking for hideouts and holes to hide safely in. They only fight when they are already captured, and by that time it's often too late.

A lion is brave, bold and full of courage and has the mentality of a hunter, not the hunted. As Christians, we are called to be bold as lions, to be directed and moved by the Holy Spirit to do the great commission, which is preaching the gospel and moving in the ministry of healing and deliverance, among the other spiritual gifts. This means we are to enter in and engage the Kingdom of Darkness, not the other way around.

DEMON MENTALITY EXPOSED

A Journal Of A Demon Deliverance Minister

There is only one weapon to be utilized to fight and win against the Kingdom of Darkness and that weapon is the Word of God, also known as the sharp two-edged sword according to Hebrews 4:12. We see even in the Old Testament, Joshua 1:8 states, "Meditate on the Word of God day and night and you will have good success. Meditating on God's Word is the key to our victory. True meditation on God's Word, digests God's Word from our natural mind down into our spirit.

It's important to know that the Holy Spirit and God's Word must become one. When one speaks the Word of God, they must be led by the Spirit of God. Many prayers have no power and anointing flowing through them, due to being merely spoken from the individual's head. It doesn't matter how eloquent and enthusiastic the prayer went forth, if it was not spoken from the Spirit of God, it will surely fall flat. This is why many are not healed and delivered.

A very effective way in meditating on God's Word taught to me by Prophet TB Joshua, is to read the Word of God slowly, attentively and repetitively. Practicing this discipline will digest the Word of God from your natural mind into your spirit, now when you speak the Word of God from the incorruptible Spirit of God placed inside each believer when they are born-again, now there is matchless, divine power.

The Holy Bible tells us in *John 1:1* that *"In the beginning was the Word and Word was God and the Word became flesh,* (meaning Jesus). So this tells us that spending time in meditating in God's Word is literally spending time communing with God.

You see when the Word of God is spoken in Jesus' Name, by the Spirit of God, the petition or command has been authorized by our

DEMON MENTALITY EXPOSED

A Journal Of A Demon Deliverance Minister

Heavenly Father through His Son, Jesus Christ. It's only now that you have a very powerful and effective two-edged sword that will put satan and his demons to flight and will break away the spiritual chains and curses of fear, sickness, poverty, sinful addictions, etc..

You might be asking, 'what does meditating on God's Word look like?' For example, let's say I'm dealing with a spirit of fear, which torments me all day long. I will pick up my sword and flip it to 2 Timothy 2:7 which tells me that *"God did not give me a spirit of fear, but of power and love and of a sound mind."*

Again I will meditate on this scripture by reading it slowly, attentively and repetitively. I will take each segment such as "God did not give me a spirit of fear." As I meditate on that, I realize if God did not give me a spirit of fear, then I don't have to have fear "But a spirit of power," I realize I have power. This is confirmed in Acts 1:8, which tells me I shall receive power when I receive the Holy Spirit." "And of love." Meditating on this, I know God's Word also tells me, that perfect love casts out all fear." 1 John 4:18. His Word also tells me that God is Love, 1 John 4:8. So if His love is in me, so is God, that by itself is extremely comforting. Scripture also tells me that my body is the temple of the Holy Spirit, 1 Corinthians 6:19, therefore God, whom the scripture says is love, cannot dwell in the same place as fear, because God's Word says perfect love casts out fear.

Jesus said my words are spirit, and those who worship me, must worship me in spirit (John 6:63).

So as I meditate on this scripture, it begins to digest out my natural mind into my spirit. Again the spirit and the Word of God must come together as one. If we say a prayer led by our natural mind or moti-

DEMON MENTALITY EXPOSED

A Journal Of A Demon Deliverance Minister

vated by our selfish desires, that prayer will have no anointing on it. This is why there are so many false religions and Christian denominations that are powerless and out of order, because they were driven by man and not by the spirit of God.

The more we spend time with God reading His Word, praying, worshiping and fasting, the more we get to know Him. When we begin to know Him, we naturally obtain a discernment to be lead by Him. There is no short cuts!!! We must spend time with God.

Lack of discernment in the Body of Christ is what has discredited the Christian church not only in the unbelievers' eyes, but also within the members. For example; an individual comes into the church with cancer, asking to be prayed for. There are some ministers who, without using any discernment, will go straight to their memory verses such as: *1 Peter 2:24, Who his own self bare our sins in his own body on the tree, that we, being dead to sins, should live unto righteousness: by whose stripes ye were healed* and *Mark 16:18, They shall take up serpents; and if they drink any deadly thing, it shall not hurt them; they shall lay hands on the sick, and they shall recover.*

They will get on the church's microphone and decree and prophesy the individual's healing before the congregation, without seeking discernment from God about the individual through prayer, but they choose to act in haste, based on their two memory verses.

Two months later the individual dies from their sickness, the person's family is devastated and many of them, along with the congregation, have lost faith in God. Many, including myself at one-time, whom had similar experiences had lost faith and even become bitter and angry towards God. This is why many have left the church and have

DEMON MENTALITY EXPOSED

A Journal Of A Demon Deliverance Minister

sought alternative solutions and false religions to life's trials and tribulations.

Now the minister might have meant well, however his declaration of this reckless faith was done in ignorance. I, myself have been guilty of this. In situations like this, it is Godly wisdom that ministers should seek discernment before making a hastily declaration. We must petition the throne according to Philippians 4:6, never demand from the throne.

God is our Heavenly Father, would it look appropriate to you to see a young child put a demand on his earthly father? That would not only be disrespectful and "bratty," but unwise. God is wise and all knowing, where does someone get off, demanding to God what is best for them and at what time they should have it?

There are many ministries preaching that God is like our heavenly servant, and that you can demand what you want by just saying Jesus' name with faith, and He and His angels will run and do it. This teaching is foolishness and in error.

DEMON MENTALITY EXPOSED

A Journal Of A Demon Deliverance Minister

TESTIMONIAL STORY

Deliverance Of An Accused Juvenile Killer

A ward accused of a very high-profile murder came up to me after a Bible study in Juvenile Hall asking to set up an appointment with me in the visiting center during the week. I told him, "I can pray for you right now if you want? "He nodded his head in agreement and we went back into the unit's classroom.

As we went inside and he sat down, a ward stuck his head in the door and said, "This ain't no joke Brah (slang for brother), this is real, this ain't no joke." The ward seated nodded his head, smiling slightly.

The ward conveyed to me that he was dealing with anxiety, fear and depression. At the time, I had no idea that he was the accused in a high-profile murder case facing a life-sentence.

I asked him if he had accepted Jesus as his personal Lord and Savior. He said "yes." I then asked if he had repented for all his sins and had forgiven anyone who had wronged or offended him. Again he said "yes." I assured him that God loved him, and that He wants him to delivered him, because He has great things for him to do.

Standing over him, I begin to pray. I start breaking the generational curses in the name of Yeshua Hamashia, and then as the Holy Spirit lead me, I proceeded to address the following spirits to manifest and be bound up-- demons of rejection, neglect, anger, murder, marijuana, e-pills, pharmakia, alcohol, demons that entered through violent and cultic video games, gangsta rap, and the demon behind his street-gang. As I begin to name these spirits, he postures up swiftly from slouching in his chair and his eyelids begin to flut-

DEMON MENTALITY EXPOSED

A Journal Of A Demon Deliverance Minister

ter rapidly. As I call out the fire of the Holy Spirit to burn these demons out of their hiding place and command God's angels to take these demons to the pit of hell, he begins to grab at his neck region, as if something is choking him.

At this time he is making gasping sounds and then it suddenly comes to a stop. I check in with him and ask, "what are you experiencing?" He replies, "Something came from my chest up to my throat and it was moving back and forth. I said, "Did you feel it leave?" and he nodded his head no. I feel prompted by the Holy Spirit, to pray that he would ask to receive the Holy Spirit, which he willingly does. I then tell him, "Let's keep praying."

In a commanding tone I say, "Angel of the Lord, put a chain of fire around the neck of this strong man (chief demon) that is hiding in his neck region, and every demon under this strong man's authority. Demons you have no more legal right, his body is now the temple of the Holy Spirit and you must go!"

I then say, "Loose his neck in Yeshua's name!" At this point, the ward's head goes quickly into his lap between his legs. He begins to gasp and choke as if something is violently choking him. I then command the fire of the Holy Spirit to torment these demons, and for the angels of the Lord to take these demons to the pit of hell. After about 10 seconds he lifts his head up quickly as if coming out of water, and breaths out, "It's out." He then smiles in relief. When I was calling the fire of the Holy Spirit in Yeshua's name, he said in a surprised tone, "I kept seeing fire when you would say that." He went on to tell me, towards the end of the prayer, he felt the demonic spirits come out of his mouth.

I told him, "say thank you Jesus," and he said, "Thank you Jesus." He then conveyed to me that he felt happy, lighter and that his head felt clearer." He then asks me, "How did you do that, how did you get that?" I told him, "It's not me, it's the Holy Spirit, and you have the same power in you, in Yeshua's name because the Holy Spirit now lives in you."

DEMON MENTALITY EXPOSED

A Journal Of A Demon Deliverance Minister

TESTIMONIAL STORY

Deliverance of Gang Leader from Demonic Tattoos

I had received an email from a Chaplain at a California jail. The email explained how a "shot-caller"(gang leader) had recently went to a Bible study and afterward, told the Bible study teacher that he wanted to be a Christian and leave his gang.

There is a process before a gang member can be placed on non-affiliate status, especially in a correctional facility, this is for security reasons. So the request was that I go out and talk to him and give the institution my observation. I was recommended based on my correctional career experience and being a certified gang specialist.

So the next day I arrive at the jail and they bring him in behind the security glass. He picks up the phone on his end, and I do likewise. I get right to the issue and ask him, "So, I was told you want to leave the gang, based on an encounter you had with God at the Bible study the other night?'

He slouches back in his chair and loses eye contact, and begins to tell me that his gang is like his family and he wasn't really sure.

I confront him, again reminding him of what he had told the Bible study instructor. He again responds by being very evasive to my question. I then abruptly stop him in a polite manner, and I say, " I believe this is spiritual, can I pray for you?"

He looks up at me, making eye contact again with a perplexed and surprised look on his face. I ask him to stretch his hand to the glass.

DEMON MENTALITY EXPOSED

A Journal Of A Demon Deliverance Minister

The first thing that stood out to me when I walked in was a tattoo on his right arm of a demon on the moon. He also had a number tattooed on him related to his gang.

Note: Tattoos can be used as portal for demons to enter into the human soul. This was the original ancient purpose for tattoos, the belief was that any symbol, name, number related to a spirit in the spirit realm, could be conjured up and summoned through a tattoo. I have called out the spirits behind the tattoos and have witnessed strange and bizarre movement under gang and witchcraft tattoos.

I then stretched out my hand towards him and begin to pray. When I said, "Fire of the Holy Ghost, I command every spirit behind the tattoos to manifest, fire of the Holy spirit burn those spirits out of their hiding place."

He begins to grab his forearms frantically, I pause and asked him what he was experiencing. He replies, "Something was grabbing my arms." He then conveyed that he felt nauseous in his stomach, as he felt things moving around.

I told him, "These are the spirits that are trying to grab you down to a fiery hell." I conveyed to him that Yehsua (Jesus) had a better life for him.

I said, 'are you ready to repent and renounce your gang?' He nodded "yes." At which time I continued to pray and command the spirits that had manifested behind the gang, tattoos among other areas to come out and go to the pit of hell. He started to move side to side as I called down the fire of the Holy Spirit.

After the prayer he told me he felt his stomach and chest heat up paranormally and spirits leaving out of him and he felt lighter afterwards and his

DEMON MENTALITY EXPOSED

A Journal Of A Demon Deliverance Minister

mood felt joyful and positive.

Email from Bible Study Teacher a week later:

Ray,

Mark ——had a Bible Study today (Sunday) in SBF and Mr. —— attended. Mark greeted him like all the others when he came in and sat down at the back of the room. Then he told Mark, who was at the front of the class, that he had visited with Rayford Johnson. Mark said he had heard about the visit, and then Mr. —— described the meeting, your praying for him and about the demonic tattoos and how he felt a heat in his chest at the time. Some inmates asked him about that, and Mark said a couple of guys then changed seats to sit farther away from him, like they might catch something from him.

Notes:

DEMON MENTALITY EXPOSED

A Journal Of A Demon Deliverance Minister

Antichrist-New World Order Weaponry
The Power Of Frequencies In Words

"Wherein in time past ye walked according to the course of this world, according to the prince of the power of the air, the spirit that now worketh in the children of disobedience:"

Ephesians 2:2

Note: You might be asking now, 'Why is Brotha Ray giving me this hi-tech information on frequency technology?' Because this is not science-fiction any more, this is real. There are government records and patents on this frequency technology that I'm about to present to you.

This technology is being deployed on all of humanity as I'm writing this now. This is the technology and weaponry of the antichrist which will help construct the New World Order, which is talked about in the book of Revelations.

I'm providing this information to help educate you on satan's arsenal, not to scare you, but to prepare you to be able to safeguard yourself and your loved ones.

The new age and the occult since B.C. have been very in-tune with the vibrations of the earthly elements, music and words. In this section I will discuss the power of the frequency of words. Most believe the talk of words and frequencies derived from the new age doctrine, when in actuality God is the creator of frequencies and words. Proverbs 18:21 tells us that: "Life and death are in the power of the tongue." Science has proven that there is power in our words, they can be actually measured with devices such as the EMF (Electric

DEMON MENTALITY EXPOSED

A Journal Of A Demon Deliverance Minister

Magnetic Frequency) Meter.

On the flip side, it has been taught to mankind by satan and his fallen angels in the ancient mystery schools of Egypt and Babylon and through books such as the Ancient Egyptians Book of the Dead and the Lesser Keys of Solomon. It is taught that frequencies are used to open up the portals of the spirit realm so one can access magical powers. Having the right frequency is the same as having the right key.

Different frequencies open and access different doors in the spirit realm. This is why the occult utilizes specific words in their incantations and spells, to open up the right demonic portals and access the right demons for the job. We see even in our earthly technology, the voice recognition system is based on frequencies. The cult has a cliche of "as above as beneath." Meaning the principles in the spirit realm and the natural realm mirror each other.

God has also given us His divine frequencies to open up his divine doors of His Kingdom and to destroy the works of satan. God's Word tells us:

He sent his word, and healed them, and delivered them from their destructions.

Psalms 107:20

That at the name of Jesus every knee should bow, of things in heaven, and things in earth, and things under the earth;

Philippians 2:10

DEMON MENTALITY EXPOSED

A Journal Of A Demon Deliverance Minister

Satan attempts to lessen God's power in mankind every opportunity he gets. For example, the name Jesus Christ, is a Greek name, in its Hebrew origin, it is Yeshua Hamashia. This divine name is not only the most powerful name in all the heavenly realms, but even in it's natural, earthly state. There is nothing wrong with using the Greek name, Jesus. There is great power in that name, even in its Greek form. I'm just pointing out the powerful revelation of the origin of our Savior's original name, Yeshua Hamashia.

The mere vocalization of the name Yeshua Hamashia brings forth peace and healing power frequencies, Let me explain: The AH sound is the most powerful sound on the planet. This is because the AH sound produces a powerful frequency of 528 hz, a frequency which is scientifically proven to heal damaged DNA of the cellular structure. The medical term is called Sound Wave Therapy. It is medically documented in one study, that in the UK, 90% of male prostate cancer patients were successfully cured.

Dr. Hashim Ahmed, who conducted the study at University College London Hospital's NHS Foundation, stated, "We're optimistic that men diagnosed with prostate cancer may soon be able to undergo a day case surgical procedure, which can be safely repeated once or twice, to treat their condition with very few side-effects."

Source: http://www.jbbardot.com/studies-confirm-sound-therapy-heals-arthritis-cancer-tinnitus-autoimmune-disease-and-more-using-vibrational-frequencies/

Satan and his network of cults have tried to replicate the sound AH in the names of their false gods and goddesses, such as: Tara, Buddha, Krishna, Allah, Shiva, Kali, Saraswati, Wakantanka, Quan

DEMON MENTALITY EXPOSED

A Journal Of A Demon Deliverance Minister

Yin, etc... along with the mantra AUM, among others.

God, who is Yahweh in the Hebrew, created the name of His son Yeshua Hamashia (Jesus Christ), Ruach Ha Kodesh (Holy Spirit) and their pronunciations for a good and divine purpose. They carry the 528 hz healing and peaceful frequency in the name, along with the Glory of God, which all the others pagan names are absent of. We see the HA sound five times in Yeshua Hamashia and four times in Ruach Ha Kodesh. It also resonates through our gospel songs in the high frequency word Alleluia (Hebrew Hallelujah).

Just anyone saying and singing these divine names from Yahweh (God in Hebrew), can produce Immediate health benefits for themselves. We serve a wise and wonderful God.

Now when God's children bandwidths God's divine names and His Word with the frequency of faith, it produces such a powerful anointing in which nothing is impossible (Luke 1:37).

DEMON MENTALITY EXPOSED

A Journal Of A Demon Deliverance Minister

———— DELIVERANCE STORY ————

Deliverance From Cancer Demon

I was working out of a Peete's Coffee, doing photography, when an elderly lady walks in hunched over and limping in pain. I was locked in on my photography work, trying not to be distracted from a client deadline I had to meet.

I then overhear an elderly woman tell the lady next to her that she had just got out of chemotherapy for bone cancer, was in extreme pain and that she was waiting for her daughter to pick her up. Out of the corner of my eye, I observed her restlessly move to another table in discomfort, hobbling and limping, moaning and groaning. It appeared she was looking out the window for her daughter.

Immediately the Holy Spirit begins to release His compassion and love for this woman, so eventually I stand up and go over to her and let her know that I'm a minister and I would like to pray for her. She smiled and said "sure."

I asked her to wait just a minute so I could backup my computer and let her know that I wanted to pray for her outside on the patio. After I finished gathering my items we went out to the patio. I sat the woman down in a chair.

The Holy Spirit gives me and word of knowledge that there was a spirit of witchcraft on her. I ask her if there was any witchcraft in the family. She tells me that she is from a Christian family in Louisiana, however her mother had deep roots in voodoo and other forms of witchcraft.

As I begin to pray standing over her, I feel led by the Holy Spirit to call out

DEMON MENTALITY EXPOSED

A Journal Of A Demon Deliverance Minister

the spirit of witchcraft and voodoo, immediately she begins to convulse from her stomach and chest region and she is grunting, what almost sounded like growling in a beastly tone.

Meanwhile passersby are looking upon this scene with intense curiosity most likely wondering what I was doing to her.

The spirit of God then leads me to call out the spirit of bone cancer and to break the generational curse of sickness, disease, and premature death. At this point the manifestation begins to escalate and then it suddenly stops. She opens her eyes as if she just woke up. She stands up quickly and says "thank you, but I'm sorry, but my daughter's probably wailing for me." She takes another step and then cries out, "Oh my God, I have no pain, the pain is gone." She begins to stomp her feet up and down, going back and forth. She gives me a hug and walks around some more, then walks off swiftly, her back straight, no more hunched back or limping.

I can't say that I can medically verify this testimony, because I haven't seen her since. Although I gave her my contact info, she never called back. All I can say is what I personally observed before and after and by the words of her own personal testimony.

DEMON MENTALITY EXPOSED

A Journal Of A Demon Deliverance Minister

New World Order Frequency Conspiracy

In 1917, the American Federation of Musicians (AFM) changed the standardization of music from 432 hz, which is a natural and healthy frequency vibration for the human body, to 440 hz (The tone "F#" in the 741 Hz Solfeggio scale, known as the "Devil's interval," is identical to "A" in standard 440 hz tuning) which is proven scientifically to be damaging to the cellular structure of the human body, which can cause both physical and emotional issues.

This was all due to the Rockefeller family, who took control over the AMA (American Medical Association) and the pharmaceutical industry in the early 1900s. This greedy Illuminati blood-line family, who is subservient to the Rothschild family, are the lead family of the Illuminati New World Order in the United States. Their focus was pharmaceutical treatment not cures, due to the fact that there is little money in cures, but truck loads of money in long-term pharmaceutical treatment.

So the Rockefellers diabolically created a system, to deploy harmful frequencies through the air waves in order to guarantee an ongoing epidemic of cellular diseases and mental disorders.

DEMON MENTALITY EXPOSED

A Journal Of A Demon Deliverance Minister

DELIVERANCE & HEALING STORY

Hearing Restored After Deafness Demon Cast Out

I was assisting my Pastor Fernando Perez at the ministry's healing and deliverance conference at the Holiday Inn Express in Sacramento, California, when an elderly Caucasian woman pointed to her right ear and informed me she wanted prayer for her right ear in which she'd lost hearing.

Before I was lead to pray healing over her ear, the Holy Spirit gave me a word of knowledge to first cast out the demon of deafness.

As I placed my hand on her ear, I begin to pray as I was lead by the Holy Spirit. I broke curses and called out the spirits of witchcraft, sickness, infirmities, sexual soul ties, new age etc.. She begins to shake and then lost her strength and went to the floor. I continued to pray for her on the floor as she's still shaking. When the last spirit left, she finally came to a stop.

When she was helped up from the floor, she locked eyes on me intensely with a surprised expression and calmly said, "My ear, I could not hear out of it, I can hear now." Her excitement began to escalate and she began to thank and praise God and tell others. God had miraculously brought back her healing to a normal level.

DEMON MENTALITY EXPOSED

A Journal Of A Demon Deliverance Minister

SIGIL MAGICK
How Symbols Are Utilized In Witchcraft

There is a spiritual practice called "Sigil Magick," which is a Cabalistic magical method whose origins can be traced back to Ancient Babylon and to such ancient texts such as the Book of the Dead and The Lesser Keys of Solomon. In this ancient dark magic ritual system, the goal is to create magical symbols and utilize patterns in tandem with movements to sedate humanity for mind control and mental enslavement. Many corporations and television networks, advertising agencies and secret societies utilize this system of magic to obtain mind-control over the masses for obedience to their objectives and profit by getting them to purchase products and services they don't even need.

The Sigil Magick process goes like this: a practitioner or magician writes down on paper a wish, spell, directive or curse with a magical intent or objective. The next step is to create the symbol, or sigil, out of the written statement. During this ritual, vowels and repetitive letters are removed and then the remaining letters are moved around to various angles and positions to create a symbol to the practitioner or magician's liking.

The next step is to charge the symbol with spiritual power or energy. There are various rituals utilized to perform the charging. Rituals range from incense, mantras, dancing, drumming, sex magic, drugs and even animal and human sacrifices.

During this process, fallen angels and demons are summoned to perform the assignment, embedded within the symbol. At this time of the spiritual charging, enhancements to the symbols will be

DEMON MENTALITY EXPOSED

A Journal Of A Demon Deliverance Minister

added, such as vibrations, colors, planets, stars, dedication to fallen angels, demons and pagan gods and goddesses are assigned to bring forth the sigil's objective. Also let me note that the practitioner can also change an existing sigil in order to deploy their desired objective.

Satan is the inventor of Sigil Magick, therefore the objectives of the sigils are always to further the advancement of the Kingdom of Darkness which includes the current development of the New World Order, which I address in the All Seeing Eye video and Sigil Magick-T.V. Mind Control Exposed, which is in the ThugExposed.Org playlist.

Sigil Magick is used in the logo of the Monster Drink. The three symbols on the can are the Hebrew numbers 6, which forms into "666," the Mark of the Beast, the antichrist's mark. Their motto is "Bring out the beast in you," which means basically to bring out the nature of satan in you. That is the objective of the sigil.

It is the belief that symbols have no real magical power over the subject, until the practitioner can take an individual from a beta state, which is normal consciousness, into an alpha state, which is an awake trance state. They believe the alpha state is the door to the subconscious or the spirit. Once it's open through the alpha trance, programming can begin. The belief is that if you can program it consistently, it will, in turn, program the conscious mind or the soul, to where an individual's beliefs and behaviors will drastically change.

So how does Sigil Magick work on it's audience?

It is the belief that symbols have no real magical power over the subject, until the practitioner can take an individual from a beta state,

DEMON MENTALITY EXPOSED

A Journal Of A Demon Deliverance Minister

which is normal consciousness, into an alpha state, which is an awake trance state. They believe the alpha state is the door to the subconscious or the spirit. Once it's open through the alpha trance, programming can begin. The belief is that if you can program it consistently, it will, in turn, program the conscious mind or the soul, to where an individual's beliefs and behaviors will drastically change.

This is where Sigil Magick techniques comes into the picture. Sigil Magick, which is utilized by all the major television networks, corporations, secret societies around the world, has the ability to manipulate the mind from the beta to the alpha state in less than 30 seconds.

Scientists have discovered that the human brain on average is regulating at 13 hz-30 hz which is 25-60 FPS (Frames Per Second) which is the beta state. At the trance state, or alpha state, it's at 8 hz-12 hz, which is optimal for subconscious programming.

Through digital television programming, the practitioner using the digital medium can input images and symbols of "Sigil Magick" into the human mind up to a rate of 200 frames per second. Remember, the mind can only process up to 60 fps, meaning the 140 + frames are poured into the subconscious mind. This overload causes the left brain in the beta state to shut down and go into a trance, or alpha, state. At this point these images and symbols, vibrations etc. are downloaded into the subconscious or spirit. Programming of the individual has begun, without them even knowing it.

The following Sigil Magick techniques are utilized to take the viewer from the beta to alpha state for programming:

Vibrations: such as beats, rhythms, harmonics etc.

DEMON MENTALITY EXPOSED

A Journal Of A Demon Deliverance Minister

Bright and flashing lights/fast flickering lights

Patterns of spinning circles and half circles and moving 90 degree arches.

Interlocking patterns

Breaking glass, a symbol cabalistic cults use for breaking through the spirit realm, or the shattering of the mind into altered mindsets, which I will talk more about in an upcoming video addressing Monarch/MK-ultra programming, which was headed by the U.S. government's CIA via the German Nazi Party.

Countdowns and Countups

Drugs & Alcohol

Pagan Dance

Now once the individual is sedated by the techniques into the alpha and trance state, the individual's subconscious, or spirit, is now open. At this point the symbol which has been charged with the Luciferian energy, releases the intended message, directive, belief, spell or curse deep into the subconscious mind which is the spirit.

Once in the spirit, these energy elements are passed on to the soul or conscious mind and the individual begins to be impacted and programmed, often without any knowledge that they are being impacted and sinfully programmed as citizens for satan's kingdom and his coming New World Order.

Once the individual is sedated by the techniques into the alpha and

DEMON MENTALITY EXPOSED

A Journal Of A Demon Deliverance Minister

trance state, the individual's subconscious, or spirit, is now open. At this point the symbol which has been charged with the Luciferian energy, releases the intended message, directive, belief, spell or curse deep into the subconscious mind which is the spirit.

Once in the spirit, these energy elements are passed on to the soul or conscious mind and the individual begins to be impacted and programmed, often without any knowledge that they are being impacted and sinfully programmed as citizens for satan's kingdom and his coming New World Order.

God has warned us about all this in His Word:

The Holy Bible tells us in Ephesians 2:2, that satan is the prince of air, which operates in those who are disobedient.

These sigil frequencies come through the air into the mind. They are in essence the fiery darts.

That's why in Ephesians 6:16 God's Word says: above all, taking the shield of faith with which you will be able to quench all the fiery darts of the wicked one.

Sigil Magick is high-level spiritual-warfare. Hosea 4:6 says "My people perish for a lack of knowledge." Proverbs 4:7, says " In all thy getting, get understanding."

DEMON MENTALITY EXPOSED

A Journal Of A Demon Deliverance Minister

UNDERSTANDING & SAFEGUARDING YOUR SOUL FROM THE NEW WORLD ORDER'S DEMONIC TECHNOLOGY & MIND-CONTROL

CERN-Opening Hell's Abyss

CERN is the modern day Tower of Babel project. The goal of the tower of Babel in Babylon was to open up new dimensions or portals to allow fallen angels to come through, to give them forbidden knowledge and the secrets to become a god or goddess. The CERN project is the largest, most epic project since the attempt to build the ancient Tower of Babel. There are over 10,000 engineers and physicists, from 85 countries, who have come to together and built a 17-mile long machine, called the Hadron Super Collider. What I find interesting is that Cernunnos was the horned god of the underworld. Do you believe it's just a coincidence that CERN is short for this pagan underworld god Cernunnos?

Basically the goal of CERN is to recreate the "Big Bang." They want to understand the particles that make up matter. One scientist explained it like this... If you studied a complex object, and you discovered that what was holding the object together was glue and you wanted to replicate the object, however there was no glue like it left in the world, and the ingredients for the glue was lost, you would have to find out what the glue was made of so you could recreate it. However you would not be able to really study the glue in its solid form. You would have to break it apart into separate particles to the ground foundation to see what it was made of in its liquid form, then

DEMON MENTALITY EXPOSED

A Journal Of A Demon Deliverance Minister

make your own glue, so you could recreate the complex object.

This is what CERN is doing, they have built the Hadron Super Collider machine, to smash particles, into smaller particles, because they want to understand how to build their own creations at will. First you must understand that this project is sponsored by New World Old globalists, who are Luciferians. They want to be like God. They also believe that smashing these particles at the speed of light opens up black holes or wormholes to other dimensions. The goal is to connect with our dimensions, which we know as the spirit realm. Connecting to the spirit realm outside of connecting to God, however, is called sorcery. This is high-level witchcraft, this is exactly what the goal was with the Tower of Babel in Babylon (Babylon means "gate of the gods"). The Tower of Babel was constructed for the purpose for the people to worship lucifer/satan and his fallen angels, it was going to be utilized as a device to open a wide portal to the spirit world, CERN's Hadron Super Collider is satan's second attempt at this. It was to connect with other dimensions, also known as creating a stargate. This is an excerpt from an article out of The Register which validates that they are planning to connect to other dimensions:

"A top boffin at the Large Hadron Collider (LHC) says that the titanic machine may possibly create or discover previously unimagined scientific phenomena, or "unknown unknowns" for instance, "an extra dimension."

DEMON MENTALITY EXPOSED

A Journal Of A Demon Deliverance Minister

"Out of this door might come something, or we might send something through it," said Sergio Bertolucci, who is Director for Research and Scientific Computing at CERN, briefing reporters including the Reg at CERN HQ earlier this week.

Source: http://www.theregister.co.uk/2009/11/06/lhc_dimensional_portals/

The theory is, if they can collide particles, they can open up black holes within the universe, in order to communicate with other dimensions through the black holes. This in essence, is the spirit realm, the black hole is the the Stargate, or door, to the spirit realm. When these black holes are open during the collisions, black matter and energy are released out of the portals, along with evil spirits. Witches, sorcerers and magicians utilize the dark matter, which is spiritual material, to create replicas of earthly creations, basically a counterfeit of God's creation, because their doctrine is for themselves to become a god.

Again this entire project at CERN was constructed on cult doctrine. In front of CERN stands a huge statue of Shiva (Hindu god), known as the "Destroyer." In the mystery religions of the secret societies it is taught "order out of chaos," symbolic of the Phoenix (A bird of Greek mythology, which after a long life, dies in a fire of its own making, only to rise again from the ashes.

From religious and naturalistic symbolism in ancient Egypt, to a secular symbol for armies, communities, and even societies. Source: http://www.newworldencyclopedia.org/entry/Phoenix_(mythology), which is a prominent symbol in many secret societies.

DEMON MENTALITY EXPOSED

A Journal Of A Demon Deliverance Minister

It is the cult's belief, that Shiva destroys, in order to rebuild. We see a consistent theme with "order out of chaos." Remember, satan wants everything under his order, when he brings the antichrist on the scene to rule the New World Order. CERN built the Hadron Super Collider machine on the LHC complex, which is situated at Saint Genis Pouilly. In Roman times it was called Apolliacum, a town dedicated to Apollyon, where a temple was built to worship the demonic deity.

Apollyon, the Greek name, like Shiva, also means "Destroyer," given in Revelation 9:11 for "the angel of the bottomless pit" (in Hebrew called Abaddon), also identified as the king of the demonic "locusts" described in Revelation 9:3-10. In one manuscript, instead of Apollyon, the text reads "Apollo," the Greek god of death and pestilence as well as of the sun, music, poetry, crops and herds, and medicine.

The name "Apollo" was often linked in ancient Greek writings with the verb apollymi or apollyo, "destroy." In a nutshell, satan is utilizing CERN as a mechanism to release his fallen angels from the bottomless pit onto earth, so they can eventually destroy mankind. They are releasing a frequency of 4,096 hz according scientific researcher Anthony Patch. Patch states:

"The 'key to the bottomless pit' is the breaking of an ENCRYPTED DIMENSIONAL CODE. One specific to Saturn's cube, requiring 4,096 qubits."

Source: http://www.anthonypatch.com/urgent-discoveries.html

DEMON MENTALITY EXPOSED

A Journal Of A Demon Deliverance Minister

God's Word references this in Revelations 9:11

9 And the fifth angel sounded, and I saw a star fall from heaven unto the earth: and to him was given the key of the bottomless pit.

2 And he opened the bottomless pit; and there arose a smoke out of the pit, as the smoke of a great furnace; and the sun and the air were darkened by reason of the smoke of the pit.

3 And there came out of the smoke locusts upon the earth: and unto them was given power, as the scorpions of the earth have power.

4 And it was commanded them that they should not hurt the grass of the earth, neither any green thing, neither any tree; but only those men which have not the seal of God in their foreheads.

5 And to them it was given that they should not kill them, but that they should be tormented five months: and their torment was as the torment of a scorpion, when he striketh a man.

6 And in those days shall men seek death, and shall not find it; and shall desire to die, and death shall flee from them.

7 And the shapes of the locusts were like unto horses prepared unto battle; and on their heads were as it were crowns like gold, and their faces were as the faces of men.

8 And they had hair as the hair of women, and their teeth were as the teeth of lions.

9 And they had breastplates, as it were breastplates of iron; and the

DEMON MENTALITY EXPOSED

A Journal Of A Demon Deliverance Minister

sound of their wings was as the sound of chariots of many horses running to battle.

10 And they had tails like unto scorpions, and there were stings in their tails: and their power was to hurt men five months.

11 And they had a king over them, which is the angel of the bottomless pit, whose name in the Hebrew tongue is Abaddon, but in the Greek tongue hath his name Apollyon.

We are literally living in the prophetic Book of Revelation. This is clearly the fingerprint of satan: "Satan comes to kill, steal and to Destroy." *John 10:10*

DEMONIC ORIGIN OF PLAYING CARDS... CAN THEY CAUSE CURSES?

Satan is a master at camouflaging witchcraft into all aspects of humanity's culture. A prime example is the deck of playing cards, often found in the average household. The deck of cards was known by the Puritans, our early Christian forefathers, as the "devil's picture book." The first deck of playing cards was created by sorcerers in 1392 for the insane King Charles of France. They were utilized by witches, psychics and satan worshipers for divinations and to cast spells and curses. They were also used as a form of silent communication. King Charles of France believed in the magical power of playing cards.

It's evident that America's mainstream obsession with magic is on

DEMON MENTALITY EXPOSED

A Journal Of A Demon Deliverance Minister

the increase. This has been successfully accomplished through paranormal television shows and movies. Disney has been the main catalyst for over 60 years in enabling mainstream America to fall in love with the world of magic. Most magicians build their shows around card tricks. The Bible clearly refers to magic as witchcraft, in both the Old and New Testament.

Leviticus 19:31 – *Regard not them that have familiar spirits, neither seek after wizards, to be defiled by them: I [am] the LORD your God.*

In the above scripture, God directly tells us not to seek after wizards. What is a wizard?

Wizard

noun wiz·ard \?wi-z?rd\ : a person who is skilled in magic or who has magical powers : a sorcerer or magician

Google Dictionary

Revelation 21:

"But for the cowardly and unbelieving and abominable and murderers and immoral persons and sorcerers and idolaters and all liars, their part will be in the lake that burns with fire and brimstone, which is the second death."

In the above scripture, it states that sorcerers will have their place in the lake of fire. What is a sorcerer?

DEMON MENTALITY EXPOSED

A Journal Of A Demon Deliverance Minister

Sorcerer

sor·cer·er

?sôrs(?)r?r/

noun

a person who claims or is believed to have magic powers; a wizard.

synonyms: wizard, witch, magician, warlock, enchanter, enchantress, magus; witch doctor; archaic mage

Google Dictionary

This scripture confirms that magic, according to God, is an abomination. Magic is the power that is conjured up from the satanic kingdom.

Many Christians and non-Christians are totally unaware of the various demonic symbolisms within the deck of playing cards. The symbolic theme of the deck of playing cards is extremely sacrilegious. The intent of its creators was to blatantly disrespect and degrade Jesus Christ.

For example, the king represents satan, the Prince of Darkness; the jack represents the lustful libertine, a pimp, adulterer, and fornicator. The 10s, represent lawlessness against the 10 commandments. The club represented the weapon of choice for murders in the 13 century, since there were no firearms. The queen represents Mary, the Mother of Jesus.

DEMON MENTALITY EXPOSED

A Journal Of A Demon Deliverance Minister

In secret, among the witchcraft network, she is called "the mother of harlots." The joker represents Jesus, known to the satanic network as the fool and the offspring of the jack and the queen.

Is Playing Cards Spiritually Safe?

I'm not going to go so far as to say that if you play with playing cards that you will instantly become demon-possessed and cursed. However, I will say that the fact remains that the origins of playing card are rooted in witchcraft, more specifically, Sigil Magick, which comes from The Ancient Egyptian Book of the Dead, the mother witchcraft book for many denominations of the occult and satanic religions going back over 2,000 years.

In a nutshell, Sigil Magick is the magical/witchcraft practice of spiritually (demonically) charging symbols, pictures, numbers, letters, patterns etc. with one or all of the following: incantations, curses, spells, mind-control, directives, and even demons.

The Ancient Egyptian Book of the Dead teaches that in order for the charge to be successfully released, an individual's subconscious mind (soul) must first be opened. In order to open the subconscious, the individual's brain frequency (brain waves) must go from their normal brain frequency of approximately 13 hz, which is the beta state, to a subconscious mind frequency of about 8 hz, which is the alpha state. Sigil Magick teaches that a brain wave of 13 hz can be taken down to 8 hz through various vibrations, beats, dancing and patterns in motion just to name a few.

This is where the magic of card shuffling comes in. A highly skilled shuffler, like a hypnotist or magician, can take the viewing subject

DEMON MENTALITY EXPOSED

A Journal Of A Demon Deliverance Minister

into a trance-like state, which can open the subject up for the demonic charge to be deployed into their subconscious, which can bring demonic curses, torment and subject one to mind control, and even demon possession/oppression.

When playing cards, individuals are focused and concentrating on the cards (whether they realize it or not) they are subconsciously focusing on the sigils on the cards and the pattern flows of the shuffling. This can involuntarily open one's soul up for the demonic, through the sigils to release their charge of demonic desires and mind control of: gambling, alcohol, smoking, adultery, fornication, greed, witchcraft, etc..., which can give root to demonic oppression and possession.

Like most of us, many individuals have been introduced to card games and card tricks since childhood, with parents believing it was harmless fun. However, satan has used this tactic to gradually condition the masses into a sinful and hedonistic lifestyle. All of a sudden, when many youth reach the age of 21, they have a strong desire to go to a casino and have drinks.

These desires didn't develop overnight–they have been gradually planted into them and nurtured by the kingdom of darkness since childhood. They have watched these images in movies, television, video games, playing card games, practicing shuffling cards, they have watched older family members exemplify an excitement and happiness about going out to the casino and for drinks. Like a serpent, satan waits very patiently for his prey, before the opportune time of attack.

DEMON MENTALITY EXPOSED

A Journal Of A Demon Deliverance Minister

DELIVERANCE STORY

Demon Deliverance of a Card Spell Victim

As a deliverance minister, I had a recent encounter with an inmate at the county jail, who was referred to me by a local pastor. The inmate informed me during the counseling session that he believed an Asian man (inmate), who was showing him a card trick, had put a spell on him. He conveyed to me that as the man was performing the card trick, shuffling the cards around skillfully in various patterns, he felt a paranormal experience of something coming over him and then entering inside of him. (Note: It is important to know that card tricks can be utilized by practitioners of magic/witchcraft to put the viewer into a trance-like state, through the pattern and motion of the movements.)

Again, this is a form of Sigil Magick, which takes the viewer from a normal brain wave pattern called the beta state, into a slower brain wave pattern, which opens the subconscious (soul). This state is known as the alpha state. Once one's subconscious is open, it is the belief that a portal to the soul
(mind, emotion and will) is created. At this time the subject can be easily susceptible to divination, spells and curses.

This incarcerated individual had developed large tumor bumps all over his back and an extreme case of insomnia to the point where it was difficult to even get an hour of sleep within a 24-hour period. He had recently been hospitalized and reassigned to a mental health unit. He told me that he was exhausted in that he was sleeping less than an hour a night and experiencing mental torment in his mind from the demonic spirits.

DEMON MENTALITY EXPOSED

A Journal Of A Demon Deliverance Minister

This large statured African-American man was practically in tears, as he explained to me this daily and nightly torment, which had been going on for months, since the "magical" card trick had been played on him.

As I began to pray for the man, I called out the chief demon behind the card spell and every demon under his authority that was causing the mental torment and sickness in his body. As I commanded the demons to manifest in Jesus' name, he began to cough profusely, with mucus flowing out of his nose and mouth uncontrollably. He began to cry and move around sporadically.

After about 10 minutes, he felt the spirits lift off of him. He conveyed that he felt lighter and happy. He then started feeling his back. At this time I had no idea that he had these tumors on his back. He then stated to me with a surprised look and excitement in his voice, "They're gone, I had these lumps all over my back and they're gone." I checked back with him a couple of times after that prayer session, and he conveyed to me that since Jesus had delivered him, he was able to sleep long and peacefully.

Hosea 4:6 states that "my people perish for a lack of knowledge" and Ephesians 4:27 tells us not to give place to the devil. This is why it's so vital that we develop a strong relationship with God through consistent prayer and the reading of His Word so we can develop a strong discernment, which will safeguard us from the pitfalls of satan as we pursue our wonderful destiny in Christ.

DEMON MENTALITY EXPOSED

A Journal Of A Demon Deliverance Minister

Our Mind Works Like a Radio

For we wrestle not against flesh and blood, but against principalities, against powers, against the rulers of the darkness of this world, against spiritual wickedness in high places.

Ephesians 6:12

A shocking report came out from a lawsuit from John St. Clair against the NSA (National Security Agency). (Evidence for the lawsuit filed at the US courthouse in Washington, D.C. (Civil Action 92-0449)-Detecting EMF Fields in Humans for Surveillance.) This lawsuit brought to the light the diabolical hidden technology of the NSA to the forefront. St. Clair states in the lawsuit that he was working for a Kinnecome Group at the NSA, Ft. Meade. They used RNM (Remote Neural Monitoring) 3D sound direct to the brain to harass the plaintiff from 10/90 to 5/91. As of 5/91 they have had two-way RNM communications with the plaintiff and have used RNM to attempt to incapacitate the plaintiff and hinder the plaintiff from going to authorities about their activities against the plaintiff in the last 12 years.

This is the technology that is currently being deployed by globalists, to condition the masses for the New World Order takeover. It's already in operation. They say that sometimes "fact is stranger than fiction." The NSA has computer technology which can detect a subject's bioelectric field code. Everyone and everything has it's own unique bioelectric field code or frequency. Just like a radio station, if the station can connect to the radio frequency of an individual's radio, then it can play it's programming as long as the radio is turned on. However, when the NSA connects to a subject's bioelectric code,

DEMON MENTALITY EXPOSED

A Journal Of A Demon Deliverance Minister

the individual can't turn off their brain. This is what RNM (Remote Neural Monitoring) is. As a believer, I know that I can block the NSA's Remote Neural Monitoring by decreeing and believing that I have the armor of God on according to Ephesians 6:11-18:

11 Put on the whole armor of God, that ye may be able to stand against the wiles of the devil.

12 For we wrestle not against flesh and blood, but against principalities, against powers, against the rulers of the darkness of this world, against spiritual wickedness in high places.

13 Wherefore take unto you the whole armor of God, that ye may be able to withstand in the evil day, and having done all, to stand.

14 Stand therefore, having your loins girt about with truth, and having on the breastplate of righteousness;

15 And your feet shod with the preparation of the gospel of peace;

16 Above all, taking the shield of faith, wherewith ye shall be able to quench all the fiery darts of the wicked.

17 And take the helmet of salvation, and the sword of the Spirit, which is the word of God:

18 Praying always with all prayer and supplication in the Spirit, and watching thereunto with all perseverance and supplication for all saints;

Scripture describes satan as the "prince of the air," and what's in the

DEMON MENTALITY EXPOSED

A Journal Of A Demon Deliverance Minister

air? Frequencies. These are the fiery darts talked about in *Ephesians 6:16*:

"Above all, taking the shield of faith, wherewith ye shall be able to quench all the fiery darts of the wicked."

The NSA has the technology to transmit video and audio frequencies into the nervous system and audio and visual cortex. Meaning, just like a television station, they can transmit an audio frequency tuned to a subject's bioelectric code/frequency, directly to the subject's audio cortex, bypassing the ears, and the frequency once into the audio cortex, will manifest the audio inside the person's head. They also perform this through video frequencies, bypassing the eyes and optic nerves going right into the visual cortex within the subject's brain, where the individual can see the programmed images from the NSA or another programmer via remote.

They can send frequencies of fear, which is an 18.9 hz frequency into the nervous system, which will increase the anxiety and heart rate, causing stress related illnesses. They can deploy a frequency of 6.66 hz, which is the signature frequency of depression, causing the subject to stay in a mode of depression, or incite a mass riot at an event or rally with a mass deployment of the 11 hz frequency,(source:http://www.whale.to/b/rifat.html), which is known to provoke violent and rioting behavior.

The entertainment industry is even in the game. They often utilize an undetected 33 hz, which is a sexual lust or arousal frequency in the music. This is why many become diehard fans of these artists and worship them as idols.

DEMON MENTALITY EXPOSED

A Journal Of A Demon Deliverance Minister

The NSA has the technology to monitor and archive all bioelectrical data of every human on the planet at any time. These computers do mind-mapping, which allows them to detect any individual on the planet's mood state and even neuro remotely send a frequency to their nervous system, brain or any other organ in their body, having the power to shut down kidneys and even cause heart attacks, etc. at will. Now this technology has made itself on the Internet market, where phone applications have been developed to decode and steal an individual's bioelectrical codes. We now have PSYOP (psychological operations) terrorists deploying attacks on humanity from the comfort of their home, in front of their home computer.

If you are a believer we are not to live in fear, stay girded up in the armor of God. Ephesians 6:12.

2 Timothy 1:7

7 For God hath not given us the spirit of fear; but of power, and of love, and of a sound mind.

This is the technology that will condition and, if need be, bully those to accept the antichrist's Mark of the Beast:

Revelation 13:16-17:

16 And he causeth all, both small and great, rich and poor, free and bond, to receive a mark in their right hand, or in their foreheads:

17 And that no man might buy or sell, save he that had the mark, or the name of the beast, or the number of his name.

DEMON MENTALITY EXPOSED

A Journal Of A Demon Deliverance Minister

Again, our mind works just like a radio. Just like a radio, our mind tunes into the frequencies we adjust to. Those frequencies either come from the Kingdom of God or the Kingdom of Satan. Those frequencies from the Kingdom of Satan causes viruses in the mind, such as sin and doubt, which programs the individual to respond and act out in fear or sin. The Kingdom of God frequencies program the individual for righteousness and to act out in faith.

This is why scripture tells us in *Joshua 1:8*:

"This book of the law shall not depart out of thy mouth; but thou shalt meditate therein day and night, that thou mayest observe to do according to all that is written therein: for then thou shalt make thy way prosperous, and then thou shalt have good success."

We Are Responsible For Monitoring What We Think

If your teenage son took the paint set you bought him and started painting demonic and pornographic pictures, would you punish him?

This is why Yeshua said if any man thinks lustfully after a woman he has already committed adultery in his heart (Matthew 5:28).

Our mind is like an art and movie studio, our mind can create things with invisible matter to form good or bad pictures, videos or sound. Many would say those are just thoughts, yes, and thoughts are frequencies, which are a measurable substance. These frequencies transmit into our visual and audio cortex to formulate pictures and moving pictures with sound.

God holds us accountable for what we create as His children, just as

DEMON MENTALITY EXPOSED

A Journal Of A Demon Deliverance Minister

the father holding his son accountable with the paint set. Our mind is a spiritual canvas, God requires for us to keep it Holy. Thoughts are a real tangible dimension in the spirit realm. Various thoughts create various frequencies which can be downloaded and viewed by spiritual beings, good and bad. Remember good or bad, frequencies always attract like-minded frequencies.

Being entertained by negative frequencies can stimulate an individual to created their own negative frequencies. For example if an individual is entertained by violent movies, this individual is more prone to create with the invisible matter in their mind, customized violent frequencies. These frequencies trigger chemicals within the brain that cause a negative reaction in the nervous system and body, which can compel the individual to create senseless acts of violence. The same holds true for the individual who wills to watch or listen to positive programming. They are more prone to create positive frequencies with the invisible substance in the brain, which will release positive chemicals in the brain, to compel them to go out and do positive acts of kindness.

Demonic spirits are disembodied spirits, which travel in the air as frequencies. *Ephesians 2:2* states:

"Wherein in time past ye walked according to the course of this world, according to the prince of the power of the air, the spirit that now worketh in the children of disobedience."

Spirits can travel in bandwidths. A bandwidth is two or more frequencies that travel in a group, such as a television frequency. It has a video and audio frequency that travels together, which then manifests when it comes through the receiver device of the television.

DEMON MENTALITY EXPOSED

A Journal Of A Demon Deliverance Minister

This is how demons are able to travel through music and television, among other devices. It binds itself into a bandwidth with the audio and video frequencies, which then enters through the individual's mind through the eyes and ears, etc.. Once inside the mind, which is part of the soul, it manifests in the body, affecting the thoughts and nervous system, which triggers the neurotransmitters in the brain, which releases chemicals that impact the physical body in a negative way.

These spirits can put their voice frequencies right into the audio cortex, so voices can be heard in the individual's head, bypassing the ears. They can place still images and video frequencies right in the visual cortex, to create lustful, frightening and all types of negative images to appear in the individual's mind. Once in, they can even gain access to the brain's pineal gland, also known as the
third eye," to open new demonic dimensions, so the individual will see, hear and interact with all types of paranormal experiences. This is the root of mental illness. Medication cannot close these demonic portals, only Yeshua can.

Within the bandwidth, these spirits can all bring demonic spiritual material, encapsulated in frequencies from other dimensions, called black matter or antimatter. This is what real magicians use to create things out of thin air with the help of demons.

It's talked about in ancient witchcraft books such as the Lesser Keys of Solomon and the Egyptian Book of the Dead. This material can be utilized to imitate anything on earth, even animals and humans. Many of what we call hallucinations were created by demons from black matter, or antimatter.

DEMON MENTALITY EXPOSED

A Journal Of A Demon Deliverance Minister

This is what they are doing at CERN a 17-mile long machine created for the purpose of opening up new dimensions: The purpose of CERN is to find the "Origins of Man and the Universe." They have stated that they want to open a doorway to another dimension.

Demons can attack the human soul and body on multiple dimensions. Remember, they are agents to construct the elements and the mind conditioning for the antichrist New World Order system. Believe it or not they can bring dark matter contained in frequencies to build structures, create and deploy spiritual weaponry etc..

Again, understand that the Kingdom of Darkness operates at multi-dimensions. Meaning demons, their weapons and structures, can vacillate from nano size to sizes larger than Mount Everest. This is why as referenced in the Holy Bible, legions (3,000-6,000) of demons can be in a single human vessel. Thousands of demons of various sizes, some which again, can be nano size or smaller, and can take over the brain, heart kidney etc.. They can bring chains, weaponry, spiritual computer devices and build structures such as walls, dams, houses, thrones, castles, etc. inside the human soul and body. I know this sounds crazy in the natural realm, but we are talking about the spirit realm here.

In the natural realm we see our body as just flesh, blood, bones, and organs, however in the spirit realm, inside the human body can look like an office building, castle or a village. When demons move in, they want to be as comfortable as possible.

Remember, in *Matthew 12:44,*

Then he saith, I will return into my house from whence I came out;

DEMON MENTALITY EXPOSED

A Journal Of A Demon Deliverance Minister

and when he is come, he findeth it empty, swept, and garnished.

During deliverance, I have individuals report back to me telling that they literally hear or feel sharp objects being pulled out of their back. For those involved in Kabbalah and the New Age, I have commanded by the spirit of God for the Kabbalah tree to be removed out the body and they literally felt a tree being uprooted out of them. When I call for the fire of the Holy Spirit, they literally feel the heat of the fire and demons coming out of all parts of their body.

You see, we are talking about spiritual things, to those who are trying to process these things with the natural mind, this may all sound like foolishness. Scripture tells us in 1 Corinthians 2:14

"But the natural man receiveth not the things of the Spirit of God: for they are foolishness unto him: neither can he know them, because they are spiritually discerned."

Think this is all far-fetched? In Kabbalah, which is the fundamental belief system of the secret societies which derived from the mystery schools of ancient Babylon and Egypt, they teach an ancient witch-craft system of deploying demonic spirits directly into the 72 parts of the brain to take over and conquer a person's mind for the purpose of mind control.

This technique is utilized by high level members of secret societies and witch covenants who are educated by ancient witchcraft books such as the Ancient Egypt Book of the Dead and the Lesser Keys of Solomon. More recently they evolved into the MK-Ultra and Monarch mind-control programs which official documents tell us were funded by U.S. government and overseen by the CIA (Central Intelligence Agency).

DEMON MENTALITY EXPOSED

A Journal Of A Demon Deliverance Minister

Why were demons deployed? Because these evil spirits often have supernatural intelligence-- they can understand the inner-workings of the brain and body from various angles and positions-- that neurosurgeons with all their high-tech x-ray and scanner devices could only dream of having.

Demons not only have a front row view of the mechanisms of the brain, but have access to the tools to place negative frequencies into the brain, to release toxic amounts of chemicals from the brain into the body, use antimatter to set up structures in the brain to cause blood clots and aneurysms, etc..

According to the ancient mystery schools, these demons, once in, claim their territory by setting up altars in their mind. These demons, which have various personalities, enter into the human mind and fuse with it, creating mental disorders. Demons are the root cause of most mental illnesses.

Again, the good news is, that as Believers, God has given us armor to deflect these frequencies away:

10 Finally, my brethren, be strong in the Lord, and in the power of his might.

11 Put on the whole armour of God, that ye may be able to stand against the wiles of the devil.

12 For we wrestle not against flesh and blood, but against principalities, against powers, against the rulers of the darkness of this world, against spiritual wickedness in high places.

DEMON MENTALITY EXPOSED

A Journal Of A Demon Deliverance Minister

13 Wherefore take unto you the whole armour of God, that ye may be able to withstand in the evil day, and having done all, to stand.

14 Stand therefore, having your loins girt about with truth, and having on the breastplate of righteousness;

15 And your feet shod with the preparation of the gospel of peace;

16 Above all, taking the shield of faith, wherewith ye shall be able to quench all the fiery darts of the wicked.

17 And take the helmet of salvation, and the sword of the Spirit, which is the word of God:

Ephesians 6:10-17

However when a Believer compromises by sinning, they can give place for these frequencies to strike and enter in.

27 Neither give place to the devil.

28 Let him that stole, steal no more: but rather let him labour, working with his hands the thing which is good, that he may have to give to him that needeth.

29 Let no corrupt communication proceed out of your mouth, but that which is good to the use of edifying, that it may minister grace unto the hearers.

30 And grieve not the holy Spirit of God, whereby ye are sealed unto the day of redemption.

Ephesians 4:27-30

DEMON MENTALITY EXPOSED

A Journal Of A Demon Deliverance Minister

This next section is about being proactive against the Kingdom of God and their advanced technological weaponry. The weaponry God has given us, trumps the Kingdom of Darkness weaponry hands down.

For the weapons of our warfare are not carnal, but mighty through God to the pulling down of strongholds;

2 Corinthians 10:14

Behold, I give unto you power to tread on serpents and scorpions, and over all the power of the enemy: and nothing shall by any means hurt you.

Luke 10:19

Notes:

DEMON MENTALITY EXPOSED

A Journal Of A Demon Deliverance Minister

——— PERSONAL TESTIMONIAL ———

Inmate-Deliverance (County Jail)

Hello my name is Robert ——— and I was once a Northerner, I'm a 40 year-old man of Christ now, that is who I serve and my code of conduct is the Holy Bible. I am now a soldier of God. I no longer have ties to any evil doings of gangs or occults.

I would like to share my testimony from then Brother Rayford Johnson, who had one day came and prayed over me, to get any satanic, demonic evil spirits out of the temple of God, which is our body, my own personal body. Now Chaplain Rayford Johnson was stretching his spiritual hand towards me and praying. I could feel something stirring up inside my stomach, back, neck, and my whole body. When Mr. Johnson kept praying in the Blood of the Lamb and demanding all the satanic demons from the Norteno gang to come out of me, I started to feel my stomach turning and moving upward to my chest to my mouth and then a loud burp.

Many of the burps came out, as Mr. Johnson demanded the demonic spirits to come out, they did as he commanded, step by step. This is the third time he has done this for me and let me tell you, it's all real, the power of God is there. First time I burped a lil and had a runny nose and from the first time I have been prayed on, I've been being molded and changed to a great man.

As now the second was even stronger. I almost threw up and Mr. Johnson wasn't praying on me, he was at another cell door and I was actually almost throwing up and spitting and burps and runny nose with tears in my eyes. And when he was done with the other inmate, I called him and

DEMON MENTALITY EXPOSED

A Journal Of A Demon Deliverance Minister

he said, 'brother you have a lot of faith, that's why you could feel the power of prayer.' And so he prayed and did it once again and oh, how I've changed my life. At one point of my life when he came to me the first time in February, in the first week of 2015, I still had one foot in with the Nortenos and one in Christ. But look brothers, I too have been through what you guys have been through. Being taught and guided the wrong direction so now I made my own choice because we cannot serve two Gods, so I decided to make my own choice and that was to step both feet with God Almighty.

Now you can do your homework about me, I was well respected in my neighborhood. A lot of people older and younger looked up to me. As if I was their idol and role model. So no matter what level you are at in your gang ties or whatever oath you took, believe me, my commanding officer is the greatest. He's the alpha and the omega, the first and the last, the beginning and the end, the almighty. I say my testimony and share to all you brothers-- there's always a way out; your journey in life doesn't end as you are now. All you have to do is want to make that change for yourself to build a relationship with Christ our Lord. It's not about being religious, it's about building a relationship with Jesus Christ.

He wants to be the one you can trust and rely on for everything you need. God is our ultimate provider! As I was once in your shoes brothers, everything doesn't have to end in bloodshed or violence. Don't be deceived into thinking that your gang is righteous in what they do. Righteous is Christ alone. Having to do others' dirty work is not right and so I myself Robert E. want to tell you that there is always a way out. You're not obligated to serve and do others' dirty deeds; you have a choice to do good or evil. The question I ask myself is, 'whose standard of good guides your life?' Man's or God's?

So now that is where I stand with God's. So I want to say to you broth-

DEMON MENTALITY EXPOSED

A Journal Of A Demon Deliverance Minister

ers, I too know what it is to be a Northerner, and believe it or not, at first it was a hard decision to make. But reading the Bible and Bible studies renews your train of thought and the loyalty to your Norteno gang stats to be more of an eye opener. And the decision finally comes to be easier as it becomes clearer that I don't want to hurt or harm anyone so you want to do good, so I finally made my decision and now my life has changed. I even came to have to submit to authority. They are just doing their jobs as if one of your family members would have a job, so now even though none of us is perfect but Christ, we all still have some flaws.

So Mr. Johnson, I do want to thank you for all you have done and for not giving up on me. As you have seen the change and that change starts with self and some inspiration of a good role model like Mr. Rayford Johnson. I've never had anyone in my 40 years of life expel demons out of me and now after, I am a new man as even my features on my face are different. This is all true and a true testimony. I now only serve God alone.

Amen

Thank you God & Mr. Rayford Johnson

Sincerely
Robert E.

Notes:

DEMON MENTALITY EXPOSED

A Journal Of A Demon Deliverance Minister

--- **PERSONAL TESTIMONIAL** ---

Deliverance of the Thuggee Spirit
Personal Testimony of David Nelson

David was a honor student and college graduate from a supportive and loving family, though despite all of that, he got caught up into the gang life, being heavily influenced as a young boy by his extended family. David was also still dealing with the tragedy of losing his older sister, who was an innocent victim in an infamous gang shootout at a Sacramento's barbershop in 2010. At the time, David was providing security for an event under the guidance of a local Freemason chapter. It appeared he was being groomed for initiation. I felt strongly compelled to talk to him about what the Holy Spirit had placed on my heart, and to ask him if I could pray for him after the event. The following is a testimony from David's account of that day:

"When he first began to pray, I started having the thought to tell him to just stop and walk away. Now I felt the strong thought and urge to PUSH him down and RUN away, but I continued to receive prayer.

He was just calling different spirits out, spirit of this, spirit that, spirit of Freemasonry, "spirits that came in through his mother's side, spirits that came in through his father's side, spirits that came in through his sister's death, spirit of premature death in his family," every time he said stuff like that, my mind would grab onto that. He called out spirit of premature death, bam! Started getting glimpses of everything that happened that I was aware of-- Uncle James died, Uncle Pat a month later, my mom's brother got killed, my sister got killed. Spirit of murder: BAM, I started thinking about the people in my family that had killed someone. More specifically, the man I'm named after, my great grandfather.

DEMON MENTALITY EXPOSED

A Journal Of A Demon Deliverance Minister

I was adamant at the beginning of the prayer that I was not going to act or dramatize anything I heard. But as he said "come out his eyes," my eyes started fluttering, I tried to justify, then he called out one and my eyes opened up completely and I looked at him. I contemplated why I had opened up my eyes all the way. After I first spoke to him in the beginning, something in me felt like I wanted to talk to him, but something else was saying, stay away from him.

He said in the name of Yeshua Hamashiach (something) and I closed my eyes back. He then told me to repeat after him and as I did, I could not understand why I felt so irritated and reluctant to speak the words. "Father…(sighing and rolling eyes) I….(irritated even more) in the name of Jesus…(wondering why I'm being like that. He kept going and my hands started to let go from one another and separate to my sides. In the beginning, I noticed he was call-ing out things like spirit of lust, spirit of greed. So he was calling out spirit that came from this, spirit of that, spirit that came through gangster rap. Then all of a sudden he said "Thug spirits!"

Unbeknownst to him, I had briefly skimmed a book in my father's room that explained the origin of the word "thug" and it's connection the Thuggee cult. When he called out the spirit, I immediately associated it with the cult I read of. My face filled with irritation and turned to the left, reacting like the class clown being called by his first name by his least favorite teacher. He immediately followed by calling out "spirits that came in from his mother's side to his father's side to the 10th generation, come out!"

I wondered as my body began to posture upright, and tried to justify it in my mind. My chest continued to rise and all of a sudden my head

DEMON MENTALITY EXPOSED

A Journal Of A Demon Deliverance Minister

snapped back, and my face rose towards the sky. (I later learned that the spirit of pride many times manifests with an upright posture, just as I had.) My mouth opened wide and I began to groan, as I felt myself no longer in control of my body. My head turned left as my shoulder rose to my jaw, and my left fist rose to the top of my left rib and began to shake violently. Meanwhile, I felt a serpent rise up the left side of my back. My body began to sway slightly, very slowly, and I tilted onto my left foot until Rayford caught me, tipping me back to balance. I continued to groan more profusely and sway like a snake against the vehicle.

My whole body swayed violently against the car. I took one last sway to the right, to the left, and to the right and my chest and face pointed to the sky as I began to (scream) in a supernatural manner, audible for over a mile, at the least. The screaming came to a halt and I felt my body release. I sat, LOL, hunched over, with my perception of reality, changed forever. I sat, speechless, contemplating if what had happened was real. With no alarm clocks ringing off to wake me out of my bed, I had no choice but to realize that what had happened was real. In the name of Yeshua Hamashia, who I had denied as being the son of God after years as a halfway Muslim, I had been delivered of a plethora of demons that I had no idea were there. He asked for the third time, "how do you feel?" I stared at him for a while before replying, "This is real; this is really real."

To my awe, he then stated, "okay, I have a few more areas I need to pray for." LOL. He started calling out this demon, that demon, demons that came in through tattoos, this demon, that demon, and he eventually called out "demons that came in through the home, come out!" My body immediately reacted, twice as violent as before, and I began to sway violently like a serpent and scream with all of my body as Ray held me from falling over and as I screamed, I simultaneously began to weep in a divine manner, tears flooding out my eyes. As I finished weeping, I

DEMON MENTALITY EXPOSED

A Journal Of A Demon Deliverance Minister

exhaled and felt ALL the weight of life, GONE!

He began to repeat "He loves you man, he really loves you. He doesn't always do this for everybody man. He did this because you have a good heart. You've got a good heart. You're humble, and you're transparent. He likes that." Then he began to pray, "Father, fill him with your peace, your love, your joy." And as he prayed, I felt something causing me to sink slowly. At first I naturally thought to resist, but as I allowed it, I just peacefully sank down the car and rested low to the ground. "He wants to use you in your family; he wants to use you to change your family. He wants to use you in counseling." He eventually said, "I sense fornication will be a temptation" and he prayed that I would receive a beautiful wife, a woman of God, that would support me in ministry. He then began to impart that I receive his (deliverance and heal-ing) anointing.

He prayed that I would receive the baptism of the Holy Spirit with the evidence of speaking in tongues. As we finished up talking, he went in his car to grab a book (Thug Mentality Exposed) he recommended to me. When I looked at the book I was shocked. I had no idea, the book he was the author of and held in his hand, was the very same book I had read in my father's room. I began to testify from the moment I left the parking lot. I received the Baptism in the Holy Spirit [with the evidence of speaking in tongues.] Seven weeks later, the Glory of God continues to manifest in my life.

DEMON MENTALITY EXPOSED

A Journal Of A Demon Deliverance Minister

Angels On Assignment

God has assigned His powerful warring angels to assist us in the deliverance ministry.

Hebrews are they not all ministering spirits, sent forth to minister for them who shall be heirs of salvation? Hebrews 1:14

God's Word also provides us understanding that angels act upon the Word of God, as directed by the Holy Spirit.

"Bless the LORD, ye his angels, that excel in strength, that do his commandments, hearkening unto the voice of his word." *Psalms 103:20*

Meaning that as I'm lead by the Holy Spirit within me, which is one with my spirit and I say, "I bind you demon of alcohol." The angels will come faster than the speed of light and bind that demon up. Then the Holy Spirit will lead me, through my mind, to tell the angels to take the spirit of alcohol to the pit of hell or the abyss, and the angels will do it. Many of the individuals who I have prayed for have told me, that they literally feel these demonic beings leave their body, sometimes even screaming in horror. Remember, there are no demonic beings that the angels can't overcome in Christ's name.

Divine Protection From Angels

I can personally testify of God's divine protection. Let me balance this message out right away and say that many Christians full of faith have been physically persecuted, martyrs for their faith. A majority

DEMON MENTALITY EXPOSED

A Journal Of A Demon Deliverance Minister

of the original disciples of Christ were sentenced to death brutally by the Greek government. Those martyrs for the truth of Christ believed it to be an honor to die for Christ. Most of these men were willing and ready to die.

Hebrews 11:35: *and others were tortured, not accepting deliverance; that they might obtain a better resurrection:*

Galatians 2:20: *I am crucified with Christ: nevertheless I live; yet not I, but Christ liveth in me: and the life which I now live in the flesh I live by the faith of the Son of God, who loved me, and gave himself for me.*

God's Word does not promise that we would be untouched in our walk with Christ, but He does promise that our souls will always be kept safe and that we can live fearless in Him.

1 Timothy 2:7

Whereunto I am ordained a preacher, and an apostle, (I speak the truth in Christ, and lie not;) a teacher of the Gentiles in faith and verity.

Philippians 1:21: *For to me to live is Christ, and to die is gain.*

This is why it's important to have that relationship with God, so that you know His perfect will for your life and you can rest in it.

I do believe, however, that while we are here on earth on our divine assignment from God, that no man or spirit can stop us. God has given His angels to protect us and our family as bodyguards. He has

DEMON MENTALITY EXPOSED

A Journal Of A Demon Deliverance Minister

also given us His Holy Spirit to empower his saints according to His will to be empowered to protect themselves and their family.

We see in scripture that David, the shepherd boy who slew Goliath, was given supernatural strength by the Holy Spirit. This is David talking to King Saul before he gets the "green light" to fight Goliath:

1 Samuel 17:36

Thy servant slew both the lion and the bear: and this uncircumcised Philistine shall be as one of them, seeing he hath defied the armies of the living God.

Psalm 18:34

He teacheth my hands to war, so that a bow of steel is broken by mine arms.

God has sent his word to protect us. Hebrews 4:12 states that the Word of God is sharper than a two-edged sword.

God's Word tells us in Isaiah 54:17: *No weapon that is formed against thee shall prosper; and every tongue that shall rise against thee in judgment thou shalt condemn.*

The Holy Bible is an actual sword in the spirit realm. God's Word tells us, that's where the real battle takes place.

Ephesians 6:12: *For we wrestle not against flesh and blood, but against principalities, against powers, against the rulers of the darkness of this world, against spiritual wickedness in high places.*

DEMON MENTALITY EXPOSED

A Journal Of A Demon Deliverance Minister

When I'm dealing with individuals who have made a decision to quit the gang and follow Christ, the biggest obstacle is fear of physical retaliation.

This is a real threat in the physical, however when we as Believers have the power to disable the violent and murderous spirit which comes against us, the Believer can render any enemy disabled with the Word of God through Yeshua's name.

I have a video on the ThugExposed.Org Youtube channel of my brother in the Lord, Sammy Dominguez titled, *Redemption of the Nuestra Familia.* Sammy was a shot caller for the Nuestra Familia, a notorious Mexican prison gang. He did 26 years in prison for murder and was radically transformed by being witnessed to through the brother of the man he killed, who was a gang rival. The brother of Sammy's victim sent a Christian couple to share the gospel with him. That lead to a series of events, which compelled Sammy to tell his gang peers that he was quitting the gang. He did this all while he was in general population, not in protective custody. I asked Sammy was he afraid. He conceded that there was a fear factor, however he stood on God's Word in Jesus' Name. He told me the main scripture he meditated on was Proverbs 16:7 which states:

When a man's ways please the Lord, he maketh even his enemies to be at peace with him.

Sammy told me that he meditated on this scripture before he met with the members of his gang. When he told them that he was leaving the gang to serve Christ, Sammy said they told him, "That's cool, but we will be watching." That was over 20 years ago. Sammy is now out of prison and serving the Lord openly, sharing his powerful

DEMON MENTALITY EXPOSED

A Journal Of A Demon Deliverance Minister

testimony. I have talked to many other former gang members, some "shot callers" who chose to quit their gang and serve Yeshua, who told me similar stories of their exodus out the gang. Like the scripture says, they were given divine peace with their enemies.

It does not matter how big they are or how many they are, when a Believer speaks God's Word from their spirit and not just from their head, there is supernatural power.

I counsel young, scared teenage boys and men who are about to enter the prison system on this topic. They fear what they have heard about sexual predators and the prison gangs and bullies.

In the physical, they truly are no match for such predators, however on the other hand, the predator is no match for the Believer, regardless of physical size who packs the Word of God loaded with Holy Spirit faith.

However many Believers, don't know how to deploy spiritual weaponry, which must be lead by the Holy Spirit, according to the Father's will.

As I explained earlier, a believer can go through various tests. An advanced test could mean turning the other cheek. Whatever tasks or assignment God sends the believer on, He will always send them equipped with faith, boldness, meekness, and most importantly love to accomplish it. We have to have the obedience, attitude and faith of Shadrach, Meshach, and Abednego, who were willing to face trials and tribulations trusting fully in God, regardless of the perceived outcome.

DEMON MENTALITY EXPOSED

A Journal Of A Demon Deliverance Minister

Daniel 3: 16-18

16 Shadrach, Meshach, and Abednego, answered and said to the king, O Nebuchadnezzar, we are not careful to answer thee in this matter.

17 If it be so, our God whom we serve is able to deliver us from the burning fiery furnace, and he will deliver us out of thine hand, O king.

8 But if not, be it known unto thee, O king, that we will not serve thy gods, nor worship the golden image which thou hast set up.

Proverbs 3:5-8:

5 Trust in the Lord with all thine heart; and lean not unto thine own understanding.

6 In all thy ways acknowledge him, and he shall direct thy paths.

7 Be not wise in thine own eyes: fear the Lord, and depart from evil.

8 It shall be health to thy navel, and marrow to thy bones.

I have personally experienced God's goodness of supernatural protection. In that he gave me, as a correctional officer, divine strength in situations to restrain and cuff inmates much larger in stature than I, after I had called on Him under my breath, during physical altercations, as I felt I was losing the momentum of my natural strength. I have also been placed in a situation where the Holy Spirit instructed me to "turn the other cheek" and I was supernaturally able to do so with a divine peace of absolutely no fear, and a mindset of humbleness, which can only come through Christ.

DEMON MENTALITY EXPOSED

A Journal Of A Demon Deliverance Minister

I have spoken God's Word boldly and directly at a group of violent thugs ready to attack me and they disbursed. I once said a silent prayer and was given an utterance to pray in tongues (my heavenly language), which miraculously brought me supernatural favor to a blood thirsty L.A. gang, ready to attack me and a friend on a dangerous street in Watts, California at night. For no logical earthly reason, in both instances, and others unmentioned, God gave me favor, to walk away in peace.

Let me now share a couple of personal stories of God's divine protection:

During a demon deliverance, a young man in his early 20s begin to growl and get violent. This individual was possessed with demons of anger, marijuana, lust, alcohol, and demons associated to his former gang (Crips). There were also demons that had come through generational curses, that came from the family bloodline, through the association of Freemasonry.

I discerned the session had the potential to escalate to an out of control situation. Being lead by the Holy Spirit, I command loudly "Angels of the Lord, bind the strong man (or chief demon) and take this demon to his knees, in Yeshua's name." This individual at the time was under full demonic possession, his eyes were rolling back into his head with just the whites showing, however by the authority of Yeshua's name he began to go down to his knees, yet reluctantly. Once on his knees he continued to resist, again compelled by the Holy Spirit, I said, "Angels of the Lord, pen this demon to the ground." Immediately he begins to go to his back with his arms and feet spread open, as if he was being penned down by an invisible

DEMON MENTALITY EXPOSED

A Journal Of A Demon Deliverance Minister

wrestler. The angel or angels held him down like this until the last demon had come out in Yeshua's name. This man testified later on video, that he literally felt an angel holding him down. He stated to me, "I lift weights and I could not move my arms or legs no matter how hard I tried."

I had been well trained in the demon deliverance ministry by my pastor and good friend, Evangelist Fernando Perez years back. Fernando was the first minister I had ever observed calling forth angels to assist him in a deliverance session. Let me share with you now my first encounter with this reality. At the time I was assisting Fernando throughout the week in doing demon deliverances on individuals, couples and families who were coming from all over California, and even the United States, to obtain healing and deliverance. We were doing the deliverances in an actual barn out in the country. It was the perfect place, because some deliverances can get very loud.

Fernando calls me up one morning and tells me that he has a deliverance to do that he believed I might find very interesting. The deliverance was on an Indian gentleman from the Fiji Islands who was extremely demon possessed. He had a history of violently assaulting ministers who had attempted demon deliverances on him. He was referred to Fernando by another minister who had heard about some amazing testimonies from Fernando's ministry.

This individual had received salvation through Christ, however was still being tormented and controlled by some very strong evil spirits. One spirit he had mentioned to us during the interview process was Kali, the hindu goddess, known as the goddess of death and destruction.

DEMON MENTALITY EXPOSED

A Journal Of A Demon Deliverance Minister

Fernando knew I would find this intriguing in that I had written a book titled, Thug Mentality Exposed. The book discusses the ancient history of the notorious thuggee tribe, and how their culture was centered around the fanatical and murderous worship of Kali.

After the interview process, my pastor went straight over to lay hands on the man in prayer while I start to video record the session. This was a large man, in width and height, who talked with a monotone voice and little to no facial expression. After about a minute into the prayer, this man begins to manifest demons and stands up growling in a loud and demonic fierce tone at Fernando as if he was about to attack him at any moment.

The correctional officer training in me brought me from behind the camera in a ready stance, prepared to physically restrain this possessed man. Fernando immediately puts his hand up to me and motions me to step back in a very calm manner. I hesitated a bit, uncertain if Fernando was correctly assessing the potential danger at hand.

He then boldly turns to the possessed man and in a commanding tone says, "Angels of the Lord, take this demon to his knees." Resisting, the man goes to his knees by the name of Jesus within seconds. Then in the same tone, Fernando commands, "Angels of the Lord put his hand behind in his back now, in Jesus' name." I see the man resisting, but again within seconds the man's hands go behind his back. At this point Fernando continued to minister deliverance to him, until the last demon left. It was very theatrical. There was intense screaming and vomiting, but praise God, that possessed man was delivered in Yeshua Hamashia's name.

DEMON MENTALITY EXPOSED

A Journal Of A Demon Deliverance Minister

Since then, I have applied this spiritual warfare technique over and over again in Yeshua's name. God's army of angels work with His believers as co-workers.

I remember recently my pastor and I went to In & Out Burger late night after a healing and deliverance conference. As we were talking in the parking lot, preparing to leave, a large very muscular, thug type man approaches us. He looks fiercely at me and asks for a cigarette. I tell him, "I'm sorry I don't smoke." He then replies to me in an a hostile tone, "I think you do!" To our surprise, he begins to walk swiftly to me in an aggressive and hostile manner, as if to assault me. Immediately a calmness from the Holy Spirit comes over me, and from my spirit I say, "I bind you up in Yeshua's name." Immediately it's like an angel slapped him, because his head and neck twisted to his right quickly, like whiplash. He then looks at me with a startled and fearful look and abruptly U-turns, walking swiftly away out of sight into the darkness of the parking lot.

God's divine protection is real for the Believer.

DELIVERANCE & HEALING STORY

Creative Miracle/"Metal to Bone"
Juvenile Hall

James, a Caucasian ward of about 17 years of age, walks into our Bible study and I ask him how is he doing. He looks directly at me with a frustrated and depressed expression on his face and replies, "I'm in pain." He points to his right side of his body and then to his wrist, which he proceeded to tell me that they had to put a metal rod in to replace the bone after his accident.

DEMON MENTALITY EXPOSED

A Journal Of A Demon Deliverance Minister

He plops down and slouches back, appearing a little reluctant about being at the Bible study. I conclude the Bible lesson plan and then we go right into the closing prayer.

As I'm praying, I feel compelled by the Holy Spirit to bind and cast out the spirits of rejection, neglect and abandonment, along with the spirit of death and sickness and infirmity.

Praying with my eyes open, while the wards' eyes remain closed, I observe James begin to tremble; as the trembling begins to escalate, he goes from his chair to the floor and balls up. He is weeping loudly and uncontrollably. The other wards, who are glancing at him, some stop praying all together. I can discern that they feel very uncomfortable watching their peer cry loudly and uncontrollably, but to my amazement none of them laughed, it's like they knew to give reverence while God was doing His work in the young man.

After about five minutes, his weeping begins to settle down. I help him up from the floor and ask him to testify to all of us what God had done for him. He begins to sob again, but he gets out, "my pain is gone, my pain is gone."

He starts bending forward and backward, then side to side. He then went to the floor swiftly and jumped into push-up position and started to do a set of pushups, then looks up at me and states as he is still sniffling, "no pain." He then gets up and points to the wrist where allegedly the metal rod was and states while he begins to cry again, "The metal is gone, I can't feel it, all I feel is bone now!!" He kept repeating, "The metal is gone, there is bone there now."

We serve an awesome God, of not only healing miracles, but also creative miracles.

DEMON MENTALITY EXPOSED

A Journal Of A Demon Deliverance Minister

TESTIMONIAL STORY

Demon Deliverance of a Suicidal Cutter

I received a call from a distressed father, who told me he was on his way to pick up his 16-year-old teenage daughter from school, because she felt like she was going to harm herself. She was a "cutter" with a suicidal history, who was on heavy psychotropic medication. At the time I received his call I was driving to another appointment. Hearing the stress in his voice, I decided to reschedule my appointment and told the father I would meet him and his daughter at their house.

When I arrived, the father opened the door and guided me to the kitchen where this pretty, petite young African-American girl was seated. Immediately I saw the slits on her wrists caused by her cutting episodes. We had a couple minutes of small talk to build a little rapport, then I got to the point by asking, "So what's going on?"

She responded by shrugging her shoulders and responding, "I don't know." I then probed deeper asking what was going on in her life. She told me she had a recent break up with her boyfriend, which sent her into a deeper depression and that she had been hearing voices in her head that were telling her to cut herself. I asked her when was the first time she started hearing the voices, she told me that she had got together with some friends a while back, and had a bad experience with some drugs (cough syrup mixture and smoking marijuana). Since that point she had been hearing voices and was having overwhelming sensations of depression come over her that were compelling her to cut herself, along with giving her a desire to commit suicide.

I explained to her how drugs work in the spirit realm, how they are used as sorcery/witchcraft to open up portals in one's soul, so they can open them-

DEMON MENTALITY EXPOSED

A Journal Of A Demon Deliverance Minister

selves up to spirits which are demons. Once the portals are open, a person will sometimes be able to to see, hear, feel, and even smell things from other dimensions which the average person cannot.

I explained to her that the word "pharmacy" actually comes from the Greek word "Pharmakia," which means sorcery, and that God had instructed us to have nothing to do with sorcery:

"There shall not be found among you any one that maketh his son or his daughter to pass through the fire, or that useth divination, or an observer of times, or an enchanter, or a witch," *Deuteronomy 18:10*

I explained to her how when she had done these drugs, she opened up portals in her soul for demons to come in. Her eyes got big as I explained this to her, I went on to tell her that an individual can also open portals to the human soul for demons to come in through ungodly music, alcohol, fornication (sex before marriage) and even pagan tattoos.

Though I knew she came from a Christian household, I encouraged her to pray the prayer of Salvation again from her heart, along with repenting and renouncing all witchcraft and fornication, among other sinful activities that she had been involved in, to assure all demonic legalities had been broken. She willingly did so, then we went to the living room, taking a high stool for her to sit in as I prayed for her.

Quickly after I started praying, she began to manifest a demon, her head started to sway back and forth and her neck began to tense up. I was literally feeling things moving around in the back of her neck.

I had started prayer by breaking the generational curses of witchcraft, secret societies, depression, suicide, sexual soul-ties among others, and calling for the fire of Holy Spirit to burn these demons out of their hiding places in

DEMON MENTALITY EXPOSED

A Journal Of A Demon Deliverance Minister

Yeshua Hamashia's name. As I checked in with her during the prayer from time to time, she said she was feeling things moving around and coming out of her head and stomach. At one point when I called out the spirit of cutting to come out in Yeshua's name, her arm lifted up and stretched out, at which time she said in a surprised voice, "Something just came out of my wrist." This so happened to be the wrist that she had been cutting on. When I felt lead by the Holy Spirit to conclude the prayer, I asked her how she was doing, she replied with a big smile, "good, I feel happy." She then explained again with excitement how she felt a demonic spirit leave out of her wrist that she had been cutting on. She went on to convey that she was feeling peace in her mind and not hearing any more voices. She then began to give thanks to Yeshua for her deliverance.

——————— TESTIMONIAL STORY ———————

Demon Deliverance Of A Martial Arts Instructor

I met with an event promoter at Peete's Coffee Shop to deliver a photo disc that he had ordered from me of an event I had recently photographed. We discussed some of the highlights of the event, then all of a sudden he began asking me questions about my gang and prison outreach ministry.

I told him some testimonial stories of demon deliverances at the jail, of those who were hearing voices and experiencing various paranormal demonic attacks. I noticed this tall, large framed man looking intensely at me as I shared with him my experiences of the power of Jesus.

Then almost mid sentence he politely interrupts me and asks, "Would you pray for me?" Other than being an event promoter, this individual was

DEMON MENTALITY EXPOSED

A Journal Of A Demon Deliverance Minister

also an expert martial artist and had been a professional bodyguard for some very prominent people. He is also a dedicated Christian, who works in outreach ministry.

I said "yes." Then I asked him why he was requesting prayer, his head nods down as if ashamed and then slowly he lifts it back up, and pauses, as if he's too embarrassed to tell me. Finally he begins to share with me that he is dealing with heavy depression, various health issues and he has been hearing voices.

I knew as one who had practiced various styles of martial arts since childhood, that most martial art studios practice in one form or another, the Eastern mysticism, such as Taoism, zen, tai chi, chi, third eye meditation, yoga, etc.. These practices are rooted in the worship of false pagan gods. These practices go all the way back to ancient Babylon. When one practices these Eastern systems, they can create portals to the soul, to give demons a legality to enter and cause mental torment, sickness and various other curses in the individual's life.

I then lead him outside to the parking lot for prayer. I have him sit on the front hood of my Prius, which puts his back towards on-going car and foot traffic.

Being lead by the Holy Spirit, I stretch my hand out towards him and begin to pray. As I begin to come against the spirits and call down the Holy Spirit fire on the witchcraft, Taoism, yoga and the demons behind the various martial arts systems he had been practicing, this big, burly man begins to breathe very fast and intensely, then begins to make a deep growling sound like a grizzly bear, rocking back and forth with his eyes closed. The growling would at times turn to moans, as if he was in pain.

DEMON MENTALITY EXPOSED

A Journal Of A Demon Deliverance Minister

When I commanded the spirits to come out and go to the pit of hell in Yeshua's name, all of a sudden he then yelled out, long and loud. Some passersby begin to stare at both him and I, most likely wondering what I was doing to him.

This same pattern would continue as I begin to break off generational curses of sickness, Freemasonry, depression and other curses and spirits the Holy Spirit was giving me word of knowledge about. The manifestations continued on the hood of my Prius for about 15 minutes, escalating at an audio level, at which I was a little concerned that the police would be called. Finally the last demon came out and he opens his eyes as if he came out of dream. He begins to look around, holding his stomach. During the prayer, he was feeling spirits move all in him.

He gets up off my car and begins checking himself out by stretching a little and then he smiles and tells me "thanks, I feel good." I convey to him to thank and give praise to Yeshua, because He is our Deliverer.

DEMON MENTALITY EXPOSED

A Journal Of A Demon Deliverance Minister

Preparing For The Healing & Deliverance Ministry

Caution: This is not a ministry an individual wants to participate in if they are not truly surrendered. They must fully surrender every area of their life to Yeshua Hamashia (Jesus Christ). There cannot be any unforgiveness or hidden unreported sin in the minister's life. These would present legalities which would give an open door for demons to enter in the minister after they had come out of the possessed individual. Let's look at the sons of Sceva: Acts 19:13-20.

The Sons of Sceva

13 Then certain of the vagabond Jews, exorcists, took upon them to call over them which had evil spirits the name of the Lord Jesus, saying, We adjure you by Jesus whom Paul preacheth.

14 And there were seven sons of one Sceva, a Jew, and chief of the priests, which did so.

15 And the evil spirit answered and said, Jesus I know, and Paul I know; but who are ye?

16 And the man in whom the evil spirit was leaped on them, and overcame them, and prevailed against them, so that they fled out of that house naked and wounded.

17 And this was known to all the Jews and Greeks also dwelling at Ephesus; and fear fell on them all, and the name of the Lord Jesus was magnified.

DEMON MENTALITY EXPOSED

A Journal Of A Demon Deliverance Minister

18 And many that believed came, and confessed, and shewed their deeds.

19 Many of them also which used curious arts brought their books together, and burned them before all men: and they counted the price of them, and found it fifty thousand pieces of silver.

20 So mightily grew the word of God and prevailed.

4-Vital Steps to Enter Deliverance Ministry

Holy Spirit: Acts 1:8

Prayer Life: "I remember a pastor saying, little prayer, little power, much prayer, much power."

Believe: (Mark 16:16-18). Faith comes by hearing, and hearing by the Word of God. (Romans 10:17)

Self-Deliverance

DEMON MENTALITY EXPOSED

A Journal Of A Demon Deliverance Minister

Conclusion:

My prayer is that you study and meditate on the information in this manual, pray about it, and have the Holy Spirit lead you into battle against the Kingdom of Darkness to do the true work of Christ, which is to win, serve and strengthen souls, by preaching the Gospel, healing the sick and casting out demons.

And he said unto them, Go ye into all the world, and preach the gospel to every creature.

He that believeth and is baptized shall be saved; but he that believeth not shall be damned.

And these signs shall follow them that believe; In my name shall they cast out devils; they shall speak with new tongues;

They shall take up serpents; and if they drink any deadly thing, it shall not hurt them; they shall lay hands on the sick, and they shall recover.

Mark 16:15-18

Please share your testimonies with us @ ThugExposed.org, by mailing them to:

ThugExposed.Org
1026 Florin Road #171
Sacramento, CA 95831

or email me @: rayfordjohnson@me.com.

God Bless You,
Rayford "Brotha Ray" Johnson

DEMON MENTALITY EXPOSED

A Journal Of A Demon Deliverance Minister

DEMON MENTALITY EXPOSED

A Journal Of A Demon Deliverance Minister

DEMON MENTALITY EXPOSED

A Journal Of A Demon Deliverance Minister

In today's fashionable Thug Culture, evil has become cool and sexy. Biblical family values have become old fashioned, judgmental and uncool. Thug Culture has obtained prominent influence through popular mainstream music, video games, television, and film. Greedy and immoral corporations are cashing in on promoting a culture which is destroying young lives physically, mentally and spiritually.

These same corporations promoting the thug mentality in the entertainment industry are investing in the private prison industry and pharmaceutical companies. The Thug Culture, made up of millions of impressionable youth have become their best customers, not in just the purchase of their products, but through the corrupting of their minds by glorifying crime, gangs, prison, drugs, and alcohol, it has manufactured more and more thugs to fill their privatized prisons in which over 40 percent of the inmates are now on psychotropic medication; for hearing voices, schizophrenia, depression, among other mental illnesses created by the harmful drugs glorified and promoted in their music.

Explore this journey through the eyes of a correctional counselor and journalist, and through the many stories of the incarcerated inmates and gang members themselves.

* You Can Purchase Thug Mentality Exposed @ www.ThugExposed.Org

Made in the USA
San Bernardino, CA
09 January 2020

62746429R00100